Trübner

The China review

Notes and queries on the Far East

Trübner

The China review
Notes and queries on the Far East

ISBN/EAN: 9783741170980

Manufactured in Europe, USA, Canada, Australia, Japa

Cover: Foto ©Andreas Hilbeck / pixelio.de

Manufactured and distributed by brebook publishing software
(www.brebook.com)

Trübner

The China review

CONTENTS OF No. 4.

THE CHINA REVIEW

ESSAYS ON THE CHINESE LANGUAGE.

CHAPTER I.
Western Opinions.

The number of those who at present speak the Chinese language in one or other of its many forms cannot be set down as much less than 400,000,000. For even if we regard the population of China Proper as greatly overrated, yet when we add to it those who living outside of the Eighteen Provinces still speak a dialect of Chinese we have a sum which is perhaps even above the total just given. And the written language of this country has a still wider use, for it is the literary and official medium of several kingdoms beyond China, each of which has besides its own colloquial idiom.

Now for a very long period the Chinese language, written and spoken, has for the inhabitants of Eastern and South-Eastern Asia embodied all that was highest in civilisation. The social and political institutions of China, handed down from age to age, surviving dynastic overthrows and popular convulsions, have exercised a great and lasting influence on the tribes which lived in the fostering shade of the Son of Heaven, and those not destined for such a blessing but dwelling in his immediate neighbourhood. In its own sphere the Chinese nation has done much though not unmixed good. In the history of the world, however, it has not played a great part, nor has it wrought for mankind the noble works which other nations have achieved. Hence its language and literature can never in lands remote from China arouse any enthusiastic interest such as that with which some of the Indo-European and Semitic tongues have been studied by our scholars, especially those of modern times.

Yet it has by no means failed to attract the attention and excite the curiosity of Western thinkers. This is only what we would expect when we think on the nature of the language and the way in which it is written, so unlike all with which they have been familiar in other languages. It was about the end of the 16th century that important and authentic information about China began to be acquired by European scholars, and their writings at that time show how it puzzled and enchanted them. The great charm at first seems to have been in its written characters. "Characters Real, which express neither letters nor words in gross, but Things or Notions; insomuch as countries and provinces, which understand not one another's language, can nevertheless read one another's writings, because the characters are accepted more generally than the languages do extend; and therefore they have a vast multitude of characters; as many, I suppose, as radical words."[*] Afterwards the richness, terse-

* Bacon, *Advancement of Learning*, Book II. (Ellis and Sped. Vol. 3, p. 399.)

ness, and simplicity of the language became discussed, and various theories arose about its origin and history. For a long time, however, little was done to bring it practically within the knowledge of Western scholars. But within the last fifty or sixty years a great impetus has been given to the study of this language. Hence we find that Grammars, Dictionaries, Translations, and works of other kinds have lately increased very quickly, though at times, it must be confessed, by a process of mere mechanical reproduction. The Science of Language also has taken up Chinese and tried to find it a place among the families of speech, with what success will be seen below.

Our Western scholars and writers who have discussed this language have held opinions about it which differ according to the point of view from which the subject was contemplated and according to the learning and prejudices of the author. In taking a short and rapid survey of some of the opinions thus held—to do which is the aim of the present chapter—it will be convenient to arrange them under three heads. These are the origin and kindred, the formal structure, and the material contents of the language, an arrangement corresponding somewhat to the classifications of languages according to their genealogy, their morphology, and their general value when compared among themselves.*

Beginning then with the origin and family relationship of Chinese, we find on this subject many and widely-differing opinions. Some have even harshly ousted it from the great clan of human tongues and left it a lonely stranger on the cold heights of isolation. Thus it was the opinion of the celebrated Golius, "a man of divine candour and a thorough Orientalist if ever there was such," that "the Chinese language was not derived from the old speech of Mortals but was constructed by the skill and genius of some philosopher"—"invented all at once

by some clever man to establish oral intercourse among the many different nations who inhabited that great country which we call China." It seems strange that a man like Leibnitz should have given his assent to so wayward a fancy and perpetuated it in one of his best philosophical works.* Within our own time also the eloquent and accomplished Farrar has refused Chinese all family relationship, and called it by such ugly names as Sporadic and Allophylian—the only connecting bond between it and any others being, strange to say, that of isolation.†

Very few, however, have clung to this heresy of the special creation of Chinese. Diametrically opposed to that doctrine is the theory which makes Chinese to have been the primeval tongue, that in which Adam and Eve talked with the Lord God, and with the Serpent, as they walked among the trees of Eden, and so the fore-mother of all other languages. One of the earliest and best known supporters of this theory was John Webb, an Englishman who lived at the period of the Restoration. His little book on this subject is full of curious learning and odd fancies, and he shows a thorough knowledge of the best works on China up to his time. Martinius, Kircher, Semedo, Trigault are largely quoted, and the author seems to have gained a very fair insight into the nature of the Chinese language. He thinks it sprang directly from Shem, whose children moved eastward in time, as Mr. Edkins also thinks, to avoid the confusion of tongues. But our Missionary Sinologue adopts the heresy which makes Ham the ancestor of the Chinese—a heresy which Kircher and others once held, but which Webb refuted. If the Chinese were allowed to choose between these rival claimants to the title of their primeval progenitor, they would most likely choose Shem as having been at least the more decent both

* See Whitney, *Language and the Study of Lan.*, p. 356 &c. (5th Ed. 1870.)

* Fourmont, *Med. Sin.*, p. xiii. Bayer's *Mus. Sin. Pref.*, p. 103 ; Leibnitz, *Op. Phil.*, p. 297 &c.

† *Families of Speech*, p. 162 &c.

in colour and conduct. Webb argues that Chinese has all the requisite characteristics of the primitive tongue, which are these, Antiquity, Simplicity, Generality, Modesty of Expression, Utility, and Brevity, "to which by some is added Consent of authors." The "plain and meek" language of Adam was transmitted to his posterity down to Noah and thence through Shem to the original Chinese. The written characters even may have been taught by one of the antediluvian patriarchs, for, not to mention earlier treatises, did not Enoch, the Seventh from Adam, leave a work on Astronomy which the Queen of Sheba possessed and of which one so late as Tertullian "had seen and read some whole pages"? The book was written in letters "significative and hieroglyphical," and no one will deny that the Chinese characters have an antediluvian antiquity, and that they are, as Kircher has it, "hieroglyphicorum in omnibus æmuli," in all respects rivals of hieroglyphics. As a clinching argument Webb writes:—"And as if all things conspired to prove this the Primitive Tongue we may observe, how forceably Nature struggles to demonstrate so much. The very first expression we make of life, at the very instant minute of our Births, is, as was touched on before, by uttering the *Chinique* word *Ya*. Which is not only the first, but indeed the sole and only expression that Mankind from Nature can justly lay claim unto." *

Many others have supposed that Chinese had its origin in the neighbourhood of that old country with the soothing name Mesopotamia. That its first speakers were the offspring of Shem seemed very probable. They had apparently a knowledge of arts and sciences beyond other tribes, and was it likely that Noah would be partial to Ham, the son who was "peu respectueux et maudit dans sa postérité?" Japhet may have had

the knowledge, but his children evidently soon lost it, as witness their long use of stone and flint tools and their slow return to more skilful appliances. But see the sagacity of the primeval Chinese. For when they left their first home to go eastward, whether when the "unaccomplishable work" which Nimrod's race began was abruptly stopt or before that event, they carried with them their "shovels, pickaxes, and trowels," along with a small collection of Primitive Roots. This is a fact which satisfactorily explains the absence of stone and flint tools from the archæological antiquities of the country. *

Most of the early Jesuit and other Roman Catholic Missionaries in China held this doctrine of the Shemitic origin of Chinese, though they did not quite agree as to which of Shem's sons was the actual immediate progenitor. There was scarcely enough proof, some maintained, to identify Yao T'ang, the first great Chinese emperor, with Joktan, the great-grandson of Shem. Some have made Ham the father of all such as speak Chinese, and others have given that honour to Japhet. Several authors have held that the Egyptian was a sister language, and others have claimed for it a relationship with Hebrew. Many also have believed that Chinese is one of the seventy or seventy-two tongues which were produced by as many angels when they were sent to the workmen in the plain of Shinar to stop the city and tower which they were impiously attempting to build. †

Edkins has tried to prove the affinity of Chinese with Hebrew and other ancient languages,—in short that it had a common origin with these "in the Mesopotamian and Armenian region"—a region to which distance alone lends enchantment. But Chinese has an "antiquity of type" beyond these others, for "being itself of the first descent

---

* "An Historical Essay endeavouring a Probability that the Language of the Empire of China is the Primitive Language. By John Webb, &c. 1669." P. 146-196, &c.

* See the *Lettres Edifiantes*, &c. T. 34, p. 217, &c. (Ed. 1832).
† Alvaro Semedo. *Relatione della grande Monarchia della Cinna*, C. 6 (1643).

from the primeval mother of human speech, we can trace in it no later elements."

This Sinologue endeavours to show also that the Chinese roots are related to those of the Aryan languages, and a distinguished Dutchman, Gustave Schlegel, has since attempted the same task in a more methodical manner. Marshman, whose defects of learning are somewhat compensated by his cautious and conscientious spirit, could not find proof enough to satisfy him of an original connection between either Hebrew or Sanskrit and Chinese. He left the question undecided, though he would perhaps have liked to see an affinity established between this language and that of Ancient India. †

The only other theory on this subject to which I shall now refer is that which makes Chinese the mother or at least elder sister of the other monosyllabic languages known as Indo-Chinese. Referring to those of Laos, Siam, &c., Marshman says—"They spring from the Chinese, however much they may have been affected by any foreign mixture, and in that language we may expect to find the origin of that simplicity of construction, which excludes every kind of inflection. From that of its descendants, therefore, the genius of the Chinese language may be easily inferred." Schott, Professor W. D. Whitney, and others have given utterance to opinions of a somewhat similar nature.‡ The old and now obsolete language of China, would probably be regarded by each of these as the common parent of all existing Chinese dialects, and of those of Cochin-China, Siam, and the others spoken of under the designation Indo-Chinese.

Turning now to the morphological point of view, we do not find here a very great diversity of opinion, and this is only what we would naturally expect. There cannot be much dispute as to the formal structure of the Chinese language and the rank which,

judged by that standard, it should have among the tongues of mankind. The first to adopt this basis of classification was, so far as I know, Frederick Schlegel, who divided all languages into inorganic and organic.* In the former division he placed (1) those without inflection and composed of roots which suffer no change whatever; and (2) those called agglutinative or affixing, in which the Grammar is formed entirely by suffixes and prefixes which are still easily separated and retain to some extent their own independent meanings. In the latter or organic division he places (3) those languages whose roots are subject to modifications from within and in which the grammatical distinctions are expressed by inflections. Chinese he puts in the first or lowest class as a monosyllabic uninflected language in which the particles denoting the modifications in the meaning of the root are single syllables having always a separate and independent existence. The Chinese roots never sprout nor yield a branch or leaf of inflection, thereby showing themselves to be merely lifeless inorganic products. A. W. Schlegel adopted and developed Frederick's classification, and Bopp, who criticises it, still goes back to the same system. He says:—"We prefer to present with A. W. von Schlegel three classes, and distinguish them as follows: first, languages with monosyllabic roots with the capability of composition, and hence without organism, without grammar. This class comprises Chinese, where all is hitherto bare root, and the grammatical categories, and secondary relations after the main point, can only be discovered from the position of roots in the sentence, &c."† So also, W. von Humboldt, who had studied Chinese to a certain extent, and had formed a high opinion of it as an instrument, regarding it as a complete or perfect language, says:—"I think I can reduce

* China's Place in Philology, p. 86, &c.
† Chinese Grammar, p. 193, &c.
‡ Schott, Ch. Sprachlehre, p. 1 & 17. Whitney, Language &c., p. 331.

* See Steinthal, Charakteristik der hauptsächlichsten Typen des Sprachbaues, p. 4, 5, &c.
† Comparative Gr., Vol. I., p. 102 (English Trans.)

the difference which exists between the Chinese and other languages to the single fundamental point that, in order to indicate the connection of words in its phrases, it does not base its grammar on the classification of words but settles otherwise the relations of the elements of language in the concatenation of thought. The Grammars of other languages have an etymological part and a syntactical part. Chinese Grammar knows only this latter."

The threefold classification of languages as isolating, agglutinative, and inflectional has been adopted by Schleicher, Max Müller, and others. Chinese accordingly with these ranks very low in the scale of languages, as indeed it must in any mere morphological classification. For English readers Farrar, whose lame learning with respect to Chinese limps slowly behind his striding eloquence, shows this at considerable length. He says that Chinese is inorganic, that it has no grammar and no words. "It differs from other languages as much as if it were spoken by the inhabitants of another planet. In this language, which, like the attempts of young children, is eminently monosyllabic and interjectional, we see, if anywhere, a picture of human speech in its primitive inadequacy."† But this system of classification has been acknowledged to be imperfect and unfit to serve as a standard for all languages.

There remain to be considered the opinions which have been formed on the Chinese language when judged by its contents and general character. Has it been declared to be rich or poor in its store of words and phrases to express the spiritual and material wants of the people? Compared as an instrument of thought with other languages, does it seem to do its work in a rude and inartistic manner, or does it seem to perform its functions well and neatly? The Missionaries and other writers on China in the 16th and 17th centuries seem to have been

quite enchanted with the great compass of this language, and the simple terse forms with which it did its work unaided by suffixes or inflections. Semedo praises even its conciseness, which makes it indeed equivocal but at the same time compendious. Such is its softness also, according to him, that when spoken correctly, as at Nanking, it charms the hearer.* Webb too says that "if ever our *Europeans* shall become thoroughly studied in the *Chinique* tongue," it will be found that the Chinese have very many words "whereby they express themselves in such Elegancies, as neither by *Hebrew* or *Greek*, or any other Language how elegant soever can be expressed. Besides, whereas the *Hebrew* is harsh and rugged, the *Chinique* appears the most sweet and smooth Language, of all others throughout the whole world at this day known."† P. Premare becomes quite enthusiastic on the subject, and he had a right to speak with authority. Chinese Grammar, he says, is for the most part free from the thorns which ours present, but still it has its rules, and there is not in the world a richer language nor one which has reigned so long.‡ And we find like high praise given to it by P. Amyot, a very accomplished scholar, who knew Chinese and Manchoo both very well. He defends Chinese from several charges brought against it, and argues for its excellences as rich and full. He regards it as peculiarly adapted for recording and communicating political science.

Coming down to later years, when the study of language began to be pursued in a thorough and critical manner, we have W. von Humboldt, as has been seen, giving great praise to Chinese. Judging from the point of view of grammatical structure one might, he says, at the first glance regard it as departing the most widely from the natural demand of speech and as the most

---

* *Lettre à M. Abel Remusat, &c.*, p. 2.
† *Families of Speech*, p. 162 &c.

* *Relatione &c.*, p. 1. c. 1.
† *An Historical Essay &c.*, p. 196.
‡ *Lettres Edifiantes &c.*, T. 33. Lettre 1. (Ed. 1724.)

imperfect. This view disappears, however, before a more precise examination. On the contrary Chinese possesses a high degree of excellence and exercises on the mental faculties an influence which, if onesided, is yet powerful.* And Steinthal, one of the latest and most philosophical students of language, speaks of Chinese as being rich in words, highly cultivated, showing in its modern literature delicacy, grace, spirit, wit, and humour. "The contrast between its means and the productions of the Chinese language is," he says, "a phenomenon quite unique in the history of language."† But the spirit of Whitney seems almost to glow with fervour when he comes to this subject. Having owned that "in certain respects of fundamental importance" the Chinese is "the most rudimentary and scanty of all known languages, he goes on—"The power which the human mind has over its instruments, and independent of their imperfections, is strikingly illustrated by the history of this form of speech, which has successfully answered all the purposes of a cultivated, reflecting, studious, and ingenious people throughout a career of unequalled duration ; which has been put to far higher and more varied uses than most of the multitude of highly organised dialects spoken among men—dialects rich in flexibility, adaptiveness, and power of expansion, but poor in the mental poverty and weakness of those who should wield them." ‡

On the other hand we find it not seldom stated that Chinese is poor in words and rude and awkward in its use of them. A Jesuit Missionary of the last century writes from Canton that there is not perhaps in all the world a language poorer in expressions, and he proceeds throughout the letter to dilate on its failings. Farrar and others have used similar phrases of depreciation, but no one has equalled Renan in bitter seathing words. Though he owns that Chinese attains its ends as well as does the Sanskrit, he says, " Is not the Chinese language, with its inorganic and imperfect structure, the reflection of the aridity of genius and heart which characterise the Chinese race ? Sufficing for the wants of life, for the technicalities of the manual arts, for a light literature of low standard, for a philosophy which is only the expression often fine but never elevated of common sense, the Chinese language excluded all philosophy, all science, all religion, in the sense in which we understand these words. God has no name in it, and metaphysical matters are expressed in it only by round-about forms of speech.†

Here ends this slight review of some of the interesting or remarkable judgments which our Western authors have passed on Chinese. It will scarcely be denied that a progress is perceptible in their appreciation of this language. But we must remember that no single stand point can furnish a fair basis for estimating its comparative value. Nor indeed is the information necessary for doing such a service yet accessible. Much still remains to be done before the genius and constitution of the Chinese language are thoroughly understood, and before its rank and value in the world's speech-tribes can be definitely settled.

T. WATTERS.

---

* Ueber die Kawi-Sprache.
† Charakteristik &c., p. 108 and 137, and elsewhere.
‡ Language &c., p. 336.

* Lettres Edifiantes &c., T. 37 p. 311 &c.
† De L'Origine du Langage, p. 195. (1 Ed.) Cf. p. 216.

THE FOLK-LORE OF CHINA.

(Continued from page 152.)

VIII.—WITCHCRAFT AND DEMONOLOGY.

The subject of Witchcraft and Demonology presents as inexhaustible a field of interesting matter as any other in the wide domain of Chinese Folk-lore. So much however has already appeared on the subject of witchcraft that, were not a full notice of popular Chinese superstitions in this respect an essential portion of the plan I have proposed, I should scarcely venture to deal at length with a matter which has already been handled with considerable ability by other pens. And indeed the following details consist more of a re-arrangement of already accessible information than of much that will be new to students of Chinese social life.

Thirteen hundred years before the birth of Christ, witches and wizards were familiar objects of Chinese superstitious respect. It is probable that they practised their occult arts at a period long anterior even to this, but the direct evidence to that effect is scanty and unreliable. Suffice it to say that the office of " Chief Wizard " was at that date a recognized appointment, and that he and his brethren exerted in those early days a powerful influence over the popular mind. They could "call spirits from the vasty deep," avert pestilence and famine and do all that is pretended on behalf of their modern successors. But scant notices of their doings however are to be found in the ancient records of the Empire. Every now and then it is related how some emperor or celebrated man resorted to the wizard fraternity to discover future events, or the means of avoiding some threatened evil. But it was not until about the third century before the Christian era that such notices were at all common. We then read that wizards existed who could summon familiars and were often consulted by the reigning potentates.

It is especially noteworthy that the hatred of witches and wizards cherished in the West does not seem to exist in China. Those reputed to possess magic powers are regarded with dread, but it is rare to hear of any of them coming to untimely end by mob violence. The more educated literati ridicule the implicit belief placed in their pretensions by the unlettered mob, but take no part in exciting it to violence, and this feeling is abundantly evidenced by the tone adopted in popular novels wherein witchcraft often plays a conspicuous part. Besides those who make a living as professed exorcists, the members of two trades—builders and plasterers—fall under a suspicion of similarly unholy proclivities. Witchcraft has always been deemed a communicable art in China. In the *Supplement to the History of the Genii* we read : " Yang T'ung Yew when a child met a Tauist priest who taught him the art of invocation and gave him a celestial writing of the three August Ones, by which he could command and subject all ghost *shên*, none of them failing to answer him instantly. Yang went down to the ninth depth of the earth to seek for the ghost of a royal concubine amongst the ghost *shên* in that quarter." Indeed the power of summoning demons is a conventional portion of Chinese supernatural tales. Thus, in a recently published translation of a popular novel entitled *The Thunder Peak Pagoda*,* we find the heroine and her servant (both originally serpents) consulting together as to how they shall raise money :

"'What then can we do?' says the mistress. 'It will be very easy for you, Madam, to find money,' replied the slave girl, 'for you are possessed of supernatural powers, and you have only to make use of some spell this evening, to enable you to procure whatever sum you may require, and by these means you will prove to him that you are truly of a wealthy family, and that you are the daughter of a high officer.' Pi-chau-niang agreed to what her servant advised, and accordingly that evening, at the third watch, she prepared seven pans of burning charcoal in a circle, and entering therein with a drawn double-edged knife, began walking round and round, muttering incantations; suddenly she uttered a loud cry, and summoned to her presence all the chiefs of the demons from the four corners of the earth, who instantly appeared and knelt before her crying, 'Your servants are present—In what can the spirits serve their mistress?' Pi-chau-niang ordered them to bring her a thousand taels of silver. Hardly had she uttered the words, when the money was before her in twenty ingots of fifty taels each."

The Chinese idea of genii can best be given in the words of their own writers.† A genie, says one, will live upon air, or even give up breathing the outer air and carry on the process of breathing inwardly, as they say, for days together as in a catalepsy (like an Indian fakeer buried alive?) He will become invisible : he will take the form of any

beast, bird, fish or insect. He will mount up above the clouds or even dive into deepest sea or burrow into the centre of the Earth. He will command spirits and demons of all sorts and sizes and have them at his beck and call. And finally after living in the world perhaps for several hundred years he does not die, for a genie is immortal, though a spirit may not be so, but he rides up to heaven on the back of a dragon where he becomes a ruler of spirits.

The Tauist considers genii as the highest class of intelligent beings and places Shên or spirits next below them : the strict Confucianist denies their existence

Like cumbrous flesh : but in what shape they
  choose,
Dilated or condensed, bright or obscure,
Can execute their airy purposes,
And works of love or enmity fulfil.
          Paradise Lost, IL., 24.

In Kwan-tzu, sec. 14, we find this definition :—" That which when it would be small becomes like a moth or a grub, when it would be large fills the world, when it would ascend mounts the cloudy air, when it would descend enters the deep—whose transformations are not limited by days, nor its mounting or falling by seasons, is called *Shên* (or spirit)."—The agreement of this with the description of genii given in the *Arabian Nights* is too obvious to need insisting on. Taoist genii (仙人) are thus described : The genie is a man who had a former existence in the world of spirits, is born into the world either on account of some indiscretion or for some benevolent object, or simply by way of amusement—usually in some lowly situation. He early begins to shew a predilection for things mysterious, to receive visitors from the unseen world, to practice Alchemy and the healing art, to prepare and use certain drugs and charms of which no one knows the use or the virtue but himself, and the more advanced genii from whom he gets from time to time instruction and assistance; and then to give up human food and all ordinary human occupation." After this there is scarcely any marvellous thing which

* 雷峰塔 *Lûi-fung Tã*, " *Thunder-Peak Pagoda*," or " *The Story of Han-wăn and the White Serpent*," Translated from the Chinese by H. C., Interpreter in Her Majesty's Civil Service in China.
† From notes kindly furnished by the Rev. J. Chalmers, M.A.

the human mind can fancy that he will not be found doing. One of the most celebrated genii alluded to in Chinese history is Chang Kwoh, who possessed a white mule which could transport him if required thousands of miles in a single day, and which when he halted he folded up and hid away in his wallet.* Another was Hu Kung, 壺 公 a magician who effected wonderful cures and was accustomed to retire at sunset to the interior of a gourd hung up at his own doorpost (See *Ch. Readers' Manual*, sect. v.) Many females also are numbered in the list of such beings, one of the most celebrated being Ma Ku 麻 姑. The seeds of the Che 芝 plant were reputed by the Taoist mystics to be the food of the genii, as were also the leaves of the Yoh Wang 藥 王 tree which grows in the moon. The result of this food is that the bodies of those who eat of it become pellucid as crystal.† As with the Westerns the genii possess the secret of a magic powder. They use the yellow heron (Hwang Kuh Ko) as an aërial courser.

The "Isles of the genii" San Shên Shan 三 仙 山 were supposed to lie pretty much where Formosa actually exists, and, like the fabled Atlantis of European superstition, they have been the subject of actual search. Su Shih or Su Fuh, a necromancer who lived about B.C. 219, announced their existence to the then Emperor, and, in accordance with his own request, was placed at the head of a large troop of young men and maidens, and set out on his voyage of discovery; but the expedition, though it steered within sight of the magic island, was driven back by contrary winds. Mr. Mayers adds to this account in his *Manual* that it is conjectured this legend has some reference to attempts at colonizing the Japanese islands. If so the parallel between the Isles of the genii and Atlantis is yet more perfect.

A very superficial comparison of Chinese and Western ideas on the subject of necromancy demonstrates their identity. The

Chinese Readers' Manual, p. 6.
† *Chinese Readers' Manual*, p. 284.

familiar stories of Jane Shore and the Countess of Soissons, accused respectively of making waxen images of the Duke of Gloucester and of Louis XIV. to compass their death; the less known account of the death of Ferdinand Earl of Derby, whose death by poison in the reign of Elizabeth was by popular credulity attributed to witchcraft, "a waxen image with hair like that of the unfortunate earl being found in his chamber and reducing every suspicion to certainty;" King James' remarks in his *Daemonology* (Book II., Ch. V.) "that the devil teacheth how to make pictures of wax or clay, that by roasting thereof, the persons that they bear the names of may be continually melted or dried away by continual sickness";—these and the host of similar stories recorded in our own and continental annals all find an exact reproduction in China.* There is a well-known legend amongst the Cantonese of a builder having a grudge against a woman whose kitchen he was called upon to repair (builders, as already noted, are believed to often practice witchcraft.) The repairs were duly completed, but somehow or other the woman could never visit the kitchen without feeling ill. Convinced that witchcraft was at the bottom of it, she had the wall pulled down, and sure enough there was discovered in a hollow left for the purpose "a clay figure in a posture of sickness." It may be noted that a reflex of the old English superstition that drawing blood from a witch renders her harmless is suggested by the Chinese belief regarding images such as that above described. Builders or plasterers are supposed to cut a gash in some part of their bodies

* The Aymara Indians believe that witches make waxen images of those they wish to injure, and stick thorns in them. They dislike any one having in his possession a portion of their body, hair, &c., such ownership conferring on the possessor the power of injuring the original owner. An Indian will pay a large sum to get back hair or other substances, which have thus passed into other hands. See *Eth. Review*, Vol. II., No. 3, p. 236.—The Chinese superstition, based on a similar belief, is that amputated limbs, &c., should be buried or burned.

whence the warm blood is injected into the interior of the image thus making it alive! Nor does Chinese superstition confine itself to clay images only. It is believed that certain wizards are able to endow with life figures cut out of paper with similar effects. In other cases these paper mannikins become the wizard's familiars and obey all his orders. There is also a widespread superstition that the feathers of birds, after undergoing certain incantations, are thrown up into the air and being carried away by the wind work blight and destruction whereever they alight.

References to necromancers who have at various times enjoyed a large amount of popular reverence abound in Chinese history, though it is somewhat difficult to distinguish between the historical "magician" and the mythical "genie." In Mr. Mayers's very comprehensive Manual are notices of, amongst others, Hsien Yuan chi, who (A.D. 847) played the part of Cagliostro, pretending to the gift of perpetual youth and the power of transforming lovely damsels into wrinkled harridans and vice versa; of Li Shao kun (Circa B.C. 110), who professed to know the secrets of transmutation and immortality; of Lu-Pan, the patron saint of Carpenters, who carved a genie which for three years inflicted drought on the people of Wu; of Lu Yen (A.D 755), who for 100 years wielded a magic sword with which he traversed the Empire, slaying dragons and emulating the deeds of the knights of Western chivalry; of T'u Yü and Yü Lui, renowned for their magic control over evil spirits; and of Tso-Tzŭ, who in the second century practised magic. It is noteworthy that throughout all this mass of legend there runs the same vein of search after the elixir of youth and the philosopher's stone which forms so prominent a feature of our own mediæval history. "Men of the four seas are all brothers," says one of the tritest and truest of Chinese apothegms; and so it would seem.

The vast extent of the Chinese Empire has allowed the natives to allot a portion of its territory to a tribe of magicians called mao shan; and it is to this country that those desirous of acquiring magical arts proceed, to place themselves under the instruction of its diabolical inhabitants. Adepts in their lore can, it is asserted, make fowls which, being placed outside houses it is desired to rob, will during the night open its doors so as to admit the robbers. Another belief refers to the existence of invisible necromancers called shan ching kwei 閃青見. People who have been deeply wronged and are unable to otherwise avenge themselves can by practising certain spells become shan ching kwei. The most efficacious way is to dig up a coffin, and, after removing the body it contains, to sleep in it for several nights in succession. At the end of so many days the sleeper becomes invisible until dawn, and can thus gratify his revenge without fear of detection.

A belief in demon monsters somewhat resembling the genii of the Arabian Nights exists in full force in China and dates back to respectable antiquity. One of the Emperors who flourished about 700 A.D., having been taken ill, dreamt he saw a blue half-naked devil coming into his palace. He stole the empress's perfume bag and also the emperor's flute which was made of precious stone, and flew off with them to the palace roof. Suddenly there appeared another blue devil, but of giant stature, having a black leather high boot on one foot, the other being bare. He had on a blue gown. One arm was like his foot, bare, with which he wielded a massive sword. His mouth was like that of a bull. This fierce looking monster seized the little one and with a blow made an end of him. The Emperor asked this monster demon what his name was. He said his name was Tsung Kwei, and that he was a military M.A. when in the body, but that now he had become a sort of colonel-commandant over all imps, ogres, wraiths, hobgoblins and the like under heaven. The emperor was greatly flattered at being visited by such a distinguished although unearthly personage, and waking up found his illness gone. He called a painter to paint for him what he had seen in his dream. It was executed so faithfully that the emperor ordered two hundred ounces of gold to be given him and that copies of the painting should be distributed throughout the whole empire, so that all the people might know and pay due respect to this blue bull-headed demon. To this day he holds a conspicuous place in the temples of the people.*

†"Although this monster demon ranked high, he was low when compared either to the ancient or present head of the vast host which abounds in the air, the earth, or the infernal regions. All mermaids of the deep, all satyrs of the forest, all needle-necked starving ghosts, the weak and the strong, whatever forms they take, whether birds, fishes, beasts or men, or a combination of some or all of them, make nondescript monsters of demons. All are said to have existed in the time of Fuhi, and even before that time under the rule of the harpy Mi Wa. She had a human face with the body of a bird. It was she who mended the visible heavens for us, but unfortunately it was not completed. There is a little hole in the north west corner, and to this day the wind from that quarter is colder than any other.

"Now we come to the present head of the demons. He was a Tanist priest named Chang Tau Ling, who lived when the kingdom of Wei was powerful. At sixty years of age, he ate the pills of immortality, after which, Lautsze, the founder of Tanism, appeared to him and gave him supreme power over all demons. When he was thus appointed to be the modern head of the demon kingdom, Lautsze gave him a book of charms and spells together with two magic swords. Chang Tau Ling lived to the age of 123 years, when he ascended in the light of day to his onerous duties of ruling the

devils. After this many of the Tanists for a time actually called themselves devils; the name evidently had become respectable.

"Having dealt on demons in general, let us now proceed to a special class of *human phenomena* which the Chinese attribute to the influence of demons. Firstly, then, is their power to produce diseases. There is no disease to which the Chinese are ordinarily subject to that may not be caused by demons. In this class the mind is untouched; it is only the body that suffers, and the Chinese endeavour to get rid of them by vows and offerings to the gods. The subject in this case is an involuntary one.

"Next come those who are possessed by the indwelling of the evil spirit. These the Chinese distinguish from the lunatics both by their appearance and language. There is more of a cringing nature in the possessed, and the patient's manner is perfectly consistent with his or her new consciousness, and which is said to be the demon's. When questioned as to his home, the demon answers, it is in the mountain or desert, generally in some cave. Sometimes he says that the person whom he had possession of before is dead, and having no abode, he takes up his quarters with a new victim. Sometimes he says he is travelling or has only come to pay a visit to a brother or sister, to a father or mother, and that after a short stay he will go away. Those possessed range between 15 and 50 years of age—quite irrespective of sex. Possession comes on very suddenly—sometimes in the day, sometimes in the night. The demoniac talks madly—smashes everything near—possesses unusual strength, tears his clothes into rags and would rush into the streets or to the mountains, or kill himself, unless prevented. After this violent possession, the demoniac calms down and submits to his fate, but under the most heart-rending protests. These mad spells which are experienced on the demon's entrance return at intervals and become more frequent the longer possessed and generally with more intensity,

---

* C. T. G., *Bogey in the Middle Kingdom.*
† The quotations which here follow are from Mr. Gardner's article. I have however taken the liberty of occasionally altering the text.

so that death at last ensues from their violence.

"A Chefoo boy aged 15 was going on an errand. His path led him through fields where men were working at their crops. When he came up to the men and had exchanged a word or two with them he suddenly began to rave violently, his eyes rolled; then he made for a pond which was by. Seeing this, the people ran up to him, stopped him from drowning himself and took him home to his parents. When he got home he sprang up from the ground several yards, manifesting superhuman strength. After a few days he calmed down and became unusually quiet and gentle, but his own consciousness was lost. It was that of another. He spoke of his friends in Nanking. After six months the demon departed, and the boy got back his own consciousness. He has been in the service of several foreigners in Chefoo since. In this case no worship was offered to the demon.

"Now we come to those who are involuntarily possessed but who yield to the worship of the demon. The demon says he will cease from tormenting the demoniac if he worships him and will reward him by increasing his riches. But if not, he will punish his victim, make heavier his torments and rob him of his property. People find that their food is cursed, and that they can't prepare any, but filth and dirt comes down from the air to make it uneatable. Their water is likewise cursed, their wardrobe is set on fire, and their money very mysteriously disappears. Hence arose the custom of cutting off the head of the string of cash that it might not run away. The 999 cash of the thousand is made to return to the one left in the following manner. The blood of a fly called Fu-chien (蚨蝉) sprinkled on the one cash left at home and the fly's eggs are put on the 999 cash that are laid out. Tradition says (and Kanghi's Dictionary perpetuates it) that the young flies in the eggs, although fastened to each cash, will all find their way back again to their mother,

bringing the cash with them. When the people's faith in these and similar antidotes fail, they yield to the demon and say, 'Hold! Cease thy cursings, we will worship thee.' A picture is stuck up on the wall, sometimes that of a woman, sometimes of a man and prostration is made to it twice a month. Being thus reverenced, money comes mysteriously *in* instead of going *out*. Even millstones are made to move in at the demon's orders and the family at once becomes rich. But it is said that no luck attends such a family; it will eventually be reduced to poverty. Even officials believe these things. Palaces are known to have been built by them for these demons, whilst the latter are obliged to be satisfied with humbler shrines from the poor."

Stories of persons being possessed by demons are so common that it is difficult to choose from the selection which offers itself. I quote the following given by Mr. Gardner as illustrating one phase of the common belief. It relates to animal possession, and is as follows:—"At Ningpo, some religions Budhist published a tract with a picture of a buffalo, a frog and a dog, and some Chinese characters. It tells how a native of Ningpo, who used to catch and kill frogs, was possessed by the spirit of his victims, how his body broke out into blotches, how he squatted like a frog, and finally was impelled to spit himself in the very manner he had spitted these innocent little reptiles."

The other story is a translation from the Chinese,[*] and runs as follows:—In Funghua district a literary man surnamed Woo had a slave girl of fifteen or sixteen who was black and ugly, but his wife was fair and beautiful. The slave always slept in the wife's apartment, till suddenly one day she was missing and could not be found for two or three days. At last an old female servant on going to fetch firewood and opening the coal-hole heard an inexplicable chirping noise and turning aside some of the firewood found the girl standing like a

* *Che-wan-luk*, Sec. xviii.

stump in the middle of it. She was perfectly inane and on being pulled out, though she walked, would answer no questions. They gave her a dose of hot ginger and water, upon which she threw up a basin full of mud. Then she began to speak and said, "There was an old man like a genie in green clothes and square cap came and called me away, the other day, I know not where. When I wanted food he gave me cakes to eat. But now I am very hungry." They gave her some rice and that night she slept in her mistress's room. But everything in the room was being pulled about, so that the master and mistress got up to look. They called the girl, but she did not answer, and as the doors and everything were in their usual state they said nothing about it. Next day the girl was missing again, and searching for her in the old place they found her exactly as before. On giving her three slaps with the hand she came to herself, but while they were in the act of scolding her lo! there was what she called "an old man like a genie" up in the eaves of the house, holding a white fan and in appearance neither old nor young but middle-aged. They went up to the room above and tried to strike him, but they could not hit him nor make him move. In the midst of the hubbub he suddenly disappeared. But as suddenly it was reported that fire had broken out in the kitchen. This was extinguished, and then all was quiet. But afterwards every night either the slave or her mistress muttered or talked in the bedroom, or else there was heard the sound of people eating, or doing something out of the way. The master did not know what to do. One day he went and got some brave men to keep guard around the room with fire-arms, but then a fire broke out down stairs, and while all the people were putting it out the mistress and slave seemed perfectly unconscious that anything was going on. Next day, when the rice was cooked, on opening the pot they found that it was all mixed with dirt, and uneatable. There was

no end to annoyances of this kind. At last they called in a Tauist priest to fast and say requiems. At the same time a "Fragrant Feast" of fine things was prepared as if for a great visitor. The master of the house put on his best clothes and also knelt down while he presented the wine and the viands: and the whole family small as well as great worshipped one whole day and night. But the trouble went on exactly as before. The genie himself would make his appearance at odd times; and in the dark there would be talking and conversation indistinctly heard, so that nothing could be definitely made out of them. One day the mistress took the slave girl, and fled with her to her (own) mother's house; and then everything was out of joint there. There were sounds and movements, and dashing and breaking of things, and clothes burning. So they fled next to a small quiet Buddhist nunnery. But bad as things were before, here they were worse; and the master was at his wits' end, all his means being exhausted to no purpose. After about half a year of this he took the girl and sold her to a villager in the neighbouring district of T'sze K'e, and his wife had peace at last. The village of Ts'ze K'e however found the girl an intolerable nuisance, and when he wanted to sell her no one would buy her; so he drove her out into the street. But nobody would have anything to do with her there either, and she turned to begging. Then her master had peace and quietness. Some say this was the fivefold permeant man who traverses the East of Chêkeang, but is never found beyond Ts'een Tang.

There are many more stories about the *Woo-tung-shên* (五通神). It appears from the Tsze-pu-yu (子不語) that in one village in Sze-chuan he required one young girl for a wife every year, and that the girl chosen became possessed by this evil spirit.

The active possession which induces a sort of ecstatic frenzy, and vents itself by bodily exertion is quite familiar to the Chinese.

Persons under this influence are known as "devil dancers," and to a great extent act the part of media for those who desire to make enquiries from the other world or induce the assistance of spirits to heal the sick. When devil dancers are called in, a feast is prepared in their honour. The head dancer, accompanied by pupils who are learning the art, present themselves at the house and having done justice to the viands provided commence by burning incense, while enquiries are made as to what is amiss. Some of the attendants then seat themselves with drums, bells, &c., and commence a sort of musical accompaniment to which the dancers keep time. Presently the music quickens; the dancers increase their speed until the whole party are almost convulsed with their efforts. Suddenly the leading dancer falls exhausted to the ground. Here for a few moments he lies as if lifeless. Presently he raises himself up and begins to speak. Questions are put to him and he describes the disease of the sick man, the remedies he ought to adopt, &c. When all the questions are answered he again falls as if exhausted, and is gradually brought back to ordinary consciousness.

Mr. Gardner states that in Manchuria "they do not ordinarily have the custom of inviting their neighbours' spirits, but the devil dancers are far better skilled in their art. The chief, with a belt of bells, stands up to dance with two of his pupils on each side. If he has not four pupils, some from the family must make up the number. The devil-dancers present many varieties and various ways of calling on the spirits. Thus, for instance, the chief says his demon is a white tiger. A whole pig must be cooked for him. He must get two children, one in each hand, to go with him to eat pig out of the boiling caldron. He assumes himself to be a tiger and thrusts his head down to his neck in the boiling water, and bites a mouthful off for his young whelp in his right hand, then a thrust and a bite for the whelp in his left hand, and finally a thrust

and a bite for himself. This over, he commences the dance. Most of the class just described are men, but there are women also who are devil-dancers. They never condescend to go about. Those who seek their assistance must go to them. In seeking their aid, the supplicant takes with him presents of incense and paper money to worship the demons, besides valuable presents of bread, red cloth, and red silks. These neither dance nor beat drums nor ring bells, but sit and commence slow shaking as from ague; then yawn, gape, and at last shake so violently that the teeth rattle in their gums; then they fall into a fit, like the former class. They tell the supplicant to return home and place a cup on the window outside, and the right medicine will be put into it by a spirit. The supplicant is at the same time made to vow that he will contribute to the worship of the particular demon, whose power and intervention they now invoke, and that he will also contribute towards some temple in the neighbourhood."

The impostors who gain their living in the way above described are of course mere ordinary mortals whose power of simulating hysteria and epilepsy easily imposes upon the masses. But the Chinese believe in the existence of a class who are human only in their outward appearance. They are supposed to be veritable demons specially sent from the spirit world to warn mankind of the consequences which may follow indulgence in evil. A Minister of State during the time of the T'ang is alleged to have been one of these demons, and legends illustrative of his powers are still to be met with in the collections of popular tales to be found in every book-stall. It does not appear that the old English belief as to witches was very remote from this demon theory. In one case we read of a witch being hunted for in a salt box, it being supposed that she possessed the diabolical power of changing her shape to any extent. But the whole subject of Western witchcraft is so wide that space forbids my even entering upon it.

It is somewhat odd to find—and one is puzzled to know whether the fact is complimentary to Christianity or the reverse—that in those parts of China to which missionary effort has penetrated, a popular belief exists in the power of Christian exorcism. Missionaries of all denominations know of cases in which either they or their converts have been called in " to cast out the devil" supposed to possess a patient. Were this to be accepted as a tribute to their powers as real intercessors with the Creator, the fact would be gratifying ; but it is to be feared that the confidence thus evinced turns rather on the popular belief that Christian relations with the Satanic hierarchy are uncommonly intimate. Be this as it may, the fact remains that converts are classed with the native exorcists. Most places of any pretension have demon shrines to which the friends of those afflicted resort in the first instance. Offerings are here made to demons of all descriptions—not merely to those which take possession of men, but to those of floods, drought* and pestilence. It is when supplications at such shrines are useless that exorcists are consulted.

Exorcists are of various kinds. Spiritualists, such as those already described, are frequently called in, their success being various. Taoist priests find more favour with some people, and their pretensions are not one whit inferior to those of the more orthodox media. Conjurors of this sort, says a writer before quoted, " sit on mats and are carried by invisible power from place to place. They ascend to a height of 20 or 30 feet and are carried to a distance of 4 or 5 li. Of this class are those who, in Man-

---

* " The P'oh of drought is doing mischief."— The P'oh is the *Shên* of drought. In the South there is a man of two or three feet high, naked and having his eyes in the top of his head. He runs like wind. His name is P'oh. Where he appears there is drought. Another name is " the Mother of Drought." It belongs to the class of elves.—*Book of Poetry*, Ta Ya.

When the *shên* of mountains and rivers caused floods or drought or pestilence they made a special sacrifice to drive them away. This was called Ying.—*Tso chuen*.

---

churia, call down fire from the sky in those funerals where the corpse is burnt. These conjurors not only use charms but recite incantations, make magic signs and use some of those strange substances which the astrologer uses to keep away evil influences." The class of so-called doctors also enjoy the reputation of being able to cast out out evil spirits, and their *modus operandi* is thus described :—" They use needles to puncture the tips of the fingers, the nose, and the neck. They also use a pill made out of *ai tsau* 艾草 and apply it in the following manner : The thumbs of the two hands are tied tightly to each other. The two big toes are also tied to each other in the same manner. Then one pill is put on the two big toes at the root of the nails and the other at the root of the thumb nails. At the same instant the two pills are set on fire and there they are kept until the flesh is burnt. Whether in the application of the pills or in the piercing of the needles the invariable cry is—' I am going, I am going immediately. I'll never dare to come back again. Oh have mercy on me this once ; I'll never return.' " All the above-mentioned practitioners may however fail, and as a last resort a professional exorcist, neither medium, priest, nor doctor, is called in. The men who follow this as a profession pretend to singular experiences. As the recognized enemies of evil spirits these latter never cease to persecute them. They are mysteriously pinched and beaten by the Puck-like emissaries of ghostly tormentors. Stones are thrown at them by unseen beings, and spirit hands seize and attempt to drown them if they incautiously venture into running water. To counteract these influences they always carry about their persons amulets of which the spirits stand in dread. Their first act when called in is to paste written charms upon the windows and doors of the room in which they operate. They then recite certain formulæ and are sometimes answered by the spirits, who promise to cease troubling the patient in future.

As with us there is a sovereign Chinese charm against witches. Sir Walter Scott, in his *Old Mortality*, refers to the popular belief that they can only be shot with silver bullets. A Chinese receipt given in the *Rites of Chow* is as follows: " If you wish to kill this *Shĕn*, take a certain piece of wood with a hole in it: insert a piece of ivory in the hole, making the form of a cross and throw it into the water: thus the *Shĕn* will die and the deep become a hill." Certain officers were in old times appointed to "hoot at," "shoot," and "kill" those spirits (*shĕn*) which were injurious.

The popular identification of the cat with matters pertaining to witchcraft in Europe is well known, and it is interesting to find that the Chinese assign to it a somewhat similar connection. As with us the vulgar believe that witches can change themselves into cats,* though the hare, and more especially the fox, are reputed to be their more

* Do you remember the German story of the lad who travelled " *um das gruseln zu lernen*" (to learn how to tremble)? Well, I, who never *gruselte* (quaked) before, had a touch of it a few evenings ago. I was sitting here quietly drinking tea and four or five men were present, when a cat came to the door. I called "*bis, bis*," and offered milk, but puss, after looking at us, ran away. " Well dost thou, lady," said a quiet sensible man, a merchant here, " to be kind to the cat, for I dare say he gets little enough at home ; *his* father, poor man, cannot cook for his children every day." And then, in an explanatory tone to the company, " That is Alee Nasseeree's boy Yussuf—it must be Yussuf, because his fellow twin Ismaeen is with his mule at Negadeh." *Mir gruselte* (I shivered), I confess; not but what I have heard things almost as absurd from gentlemen and ladies in Europe ; but an " extravagance " in a *kuflan* has quite a different effect from one in a tail-coat. " What ! my butcher's boy who brings the meat—a cat ! " I gasped. " To be sure, and he knows well where to look for a bit of good cookery, you see. All twins go out as cats at night, if they go to sleep hungry ; and their own bodies lie at home like dead meanwhile, but no one must touch them, or they would die. When they grow up to ten or twelve they leave it off. Why, your own boy Achmet does it. Oh, Achmet ! " Achmet appears. " Boy, don't you go out as a cat at night ? " " No," said Achmet, tranquilly, " I am not a twin—my sister's sons do." I inquired if people were not afraid of such cats. " No, there is no fear, they only eat a little of the cookery ; but if you beat them they will tell their parents, next day, ' So and so beat me in his

favourite disguises. But the demoniacal attributes of a cat's ghost are more singular. In Section I, of the Che Wĕn Luh (誌聞錄) occurs the following notice† : " At Leong Chow in the province of Kansuh the people sometimes do homage to the ghost of a cat. The same thing is mentioned in the history of the North. The way they proceed with this monstrous thing is first to hang the cat, and then perform certain ceremonies of fasting and requiems for seven weeks, when the spiritual communication is established. This is afterwards transferred to a wooden tablet, and put up behind the door, where the owner of the cat honours it with offerings. By the side of it is placed a bag about five inches long, intended for the cat's use. From time to time it goes and steals people's things, and then, about the fourth watch of the night before cock crowing, the bag is amissing. After a little while it is hung up on the corner of the house, and the person uses a ladder to fetch it down. When the mouth of the bag is opened, and the bag inverted over a chest, as much as two hundred catties of rice or peas are got out of it, so much does the depraved imp manage to make the little space hold. Those who serve it always get rich very fast."

A certain prefect once received a birthday present of rice from a friend. It was over a thousand catties and was put into a large cask. Several days after the prefect sent a man to divide it out, when it was noticed that the top of the flour was all in a crust like paper, and below it was clean gone.

house last night,' and show their bruises. No, they are not Afreets ; they are *beni Adam* ; only twins do it, and if you give them a sort of onion broth and camel's milk the first thing when they are born, they don't do it at all." Omar professed never to have heard it, but I am sure he had, only he dreads being laughed at. One of the American missionaries told me something like it, as belonging to the Copts, but it is entirely Egyptian, and common to both religions. I asked several Copts, who assured me it was true, and told it just the same. Is it a remnant of the doctrine of transmigration ? However, the notion fully accounts for the horror the people feel at the idea of killing a cat.—*Lady Duff Gordon's Last Letters.*

† Chalmers.

The man, in a fright, told the prefect, who sent an officer to enquire into the matter. It was then found that behind the prefect's residence there was a person who practised sacrificing to this kind of cat. The officer found out the image and severely chastised it in the hall with 40 blows, and also flogged its owner. He then laughed and sent them off. After this, as the story goes, the Shin had no efficacy, and the affair was at an end. Choo-tzu says—"The spirituousness (Ling) of Shên is the result of the accumulated earnestness of the people—there is really no Shên. When one turns his back upon it the spirituousness is immediately dispersed. Therefore while the people honor it the Shin keeps its place, but you may scatter it with a kick."

Tigers also figure as demoniacs or ghosts. In the same work as that above quoted from a story relates how a benighted traveller suddenly observed amongst the brushwood a brilliant light and a man in red clothes, with a golden crown and armour of rare brightness, and before and behind him a regular retinue of followers escorting him along. The traveller was astonished, and, wondering what mandarin it could be, hid himself in the wood. Next day he asked the natives of the place who it could have been. They told him it was the tiger ghost of the mountains. "When he wishes to eat people up he puts off his clothes and is changed into a striped tiger. He then advances with a great roar and the traveller is instantly torn in pieces." "You," said they, "have had a wonderful escape."

Nor are tigers alone in this regard. The ghosts of the "green ox" and "black fowl"* are mentioned in native legends; while a yet more fantastic extract narrates that "the carp as soon as its scales number 360 is caught and carried away by dragons; but if every year a shên be placed to guard it, it cannot be carried away. This shên is a tortoise.†

* 談徵 (T'an ch'ing.) Sec. IV.
† 述異記 Shuh E Ké.

Dragons again furnish their quota of ghostly representatives, and the following legend accounts for the popular belief. During the reign of an emperor of the T'ang dynasty, the dragon god of rain had greatly offended the great high god, and orders were consequently given to the prime minister to behead him on such and such a day. On the night before the execution, the dragon god of rain appeared in a dream to the Emperor and begged him to intercede on his behalf and exercise his influence over his minister. The Emperor promised he would. The following day the Emperor invited his minister to play chess with him. He hoped he would forget the time, and thus the dragon god would be free. As the hour drew nigh the minister got very sleepy. The Emperor seeing this, did not mention a word about the dragon god, but let the minister sleep. Suddenly, the latter jumped up and said, "I must behead,—I must behead immediately;" and right between them a dragon's head fell from the sky. The King fell back with fright and was taken ill. That night the dragon's ghost appeared to him in a dream and threatened him severely for this breach of promise, insisting on bringing the case up before the judge of the lower regions. The Emperor explained, begged forgiveness and made a promise, the results of which remain to this day. He engaged to honour the dragon god by having all his high officers and the great people of the land to carry the dragon above their heads. The plan adopted was to place a dragon's head on every palace roof so that when the gentry and officials were at home, they had a dragon's head over them. The head seen so often on temples and palaces is said to have had this origin."* In those days, adds the account from which the foregoing is quoted, the demons had such unlimited power to transform themselves that a son would not leave his father, or a husband his wife, without secret tickets, which they carried about with them and

* C. T. Gardner.

compared on meeting. If unable to produce the ticket he was believed to be a demon in human form. This is the origin of the proverb: "If your ticket be lost, you are hopeless."

But of all known animals the fox plays the principle part in Chinese demonology. European folk-lore assigns a prominent place to the were-wolves (Germ. *Wehrwolf*, Port. *Lobis-homem*), which are even now believed by the superstitious peasantry of many countries to haunt their native forests. Well, in China we find the same idea in a slightly different form. The fox takes the place of the wolf, and "fairy foxes" play an important part in every native collection of supernatural tales. The belief in their existence dates from remote antiquity, though more prevalent in Northern than in Southern China, the inhabitants of the latter taking the doings of genii more especially as the basis of their fairy lore. There is how-ever this difference between the were-wolf and the fairy fox:—that whereas the former is invariably malicious, the latter may be either beneficent or malignant. In many of the tales the fox is only transformed (as in the well-known nursery story of "Beauty and the Beast") into human shape *after* making acquaintance with its host. "At the age of 50 the fox can take the form of a woman, and at that of 100 can assume the appearance of a young and beautiful girl. When 1000 years old he is admitted to the heavens and becomes the celestial fox."[*]

In and about Peking the belief in foxes having power to assume a human shape flourishes perhaps more thoroughly than in any other part of the empire, though similar stories are told throughout the eighteen provinces. The *Liao-chai-chih-yi* (聊齋志異), a collection of tales published in 1765, abounds with narrations of this nature, many of the most curious, unfortunately, being unsuitable for publication in an English dress. But the whole subject has

[*] *Chinese Readers' Manual*, p. 61.

been so fully dealt with in accessible publi-cations that the extended notice which the subject would permit is unnecessary. Dr. Birch, of the British Museum, wrote an interesting paper on the subject of Fairy Foxes[*] in No. III., of the *Chinese and Ja-panese Repository* (1863), which was followed by a notice from the pen of the well-known sinologue Mr. W. F. Mayers, in No. III., of Vol. I., of *Notes and Queries on China and Japan* (1867). The most complete essay on the subject, however, which has yet appeared was written by Mr. T. Watters, and read before the North China Branch of the Royal Asiatic Society in March 1873. That ac-curate and painstaking scholar thus opens his remarks on the subject:—

"Chinese philosophers seem to be agreed in attributing to Reynard a long life, some making the number of his years 800 and others extending it even to a thousand. This power of prolonging life they suppose to result from the animal's living in caves and holes where it is shut out from the sun. The vital powers can thus operate free from disturbance and the wearing effect of the sun's heat and light. The fox, badger, mole and some other cave-dwelling animals are all grouped together as enjoying long life. The Chinese are not alone in thus regarding the exclusion of light and air as tending to prolong existence. Not to refer

[*] A specimen of the still pervading supersti-tion respecting the Fox, comes from Minato-mura, in Ibaraki Ken, Japan. A man found a fox's hole in his garden. At the same time his wife dreamt that she had seen a fox whom she was satisfied was none other than Inari-sama. Full of dread, the man put this and that together, and came to the conclusion that the hole must be the abode of Inari-sama, and he forthwith had a small temple put up over it. He then called for the Shinto priest; and after much ado, the matter got abroad, and crowds came to worship at this temple. At last the Saibansho officials of the Ken heard of what was going on, and sent for the man and his wife. The interview must have been somewhat disappointing to them, for the judges told them such superstitions now became criminal; and the punishment due for such follies was 40 days' imprisonment. As, however, in this instance, it was clearly the result of extreme ignorance on the part of the interesting pair, they were let off with a fine of 3 yen.

to others, our own Bacon says:—' A life in caves and holes, where the rays of the sun do not enter, may perhaps tend to longevity; for the air of itself unexcited by heat has not much power to prey upon the body. Certainly on looking back, it appears from many remains and monuments that the size and stature of men were anciently much greater than they had been since, as in Sicily and some other places ; and such men generally lived in caves. Now there is some affinity between length of age and largeness of limbs. The cave of Epimenides likewise passes current among the fables.' "

The use of the several parts of the fox's body in the Chinese pharmacopeia is followed by an account of the Chinese opinion of his cunning, in which we read as follows :—

" Like most Western nations the Chinese ascribe to the fox a cunning, crafty disposition by which he can disarm suspicion on the part of the very animals which constitute his prey. . . . . The notion about the fox's caution is put to practical use in the North of China, for it has been observed that when he is crossing a frozen river or lake he advances very slowly and deliberately, putting his head down close to the ice and listening for the sound of water beneath. Accordingly when in the early spring the traveller fears the stability of the ice, if he observes on its surface traces of the fox's footsteps he may proceed without any apprehension. One can easily see what an opportunity is presented here again to the Chinese mind for the exercise of myth-making ingenuity. Below the ice is the region of the *Yin* or female element—the dark world of death and obscurity—while above it is the region of the *Yang* or male element—the bright world of life and activity. Accordingly it has come to pass that the fox is represented as living on the debatable land which is neither the earth of life nor the Hades of death. His dwelling place on the earth is among the tombs, or actually, rather, within the tomb, and the spirits of the deceased often occupy the body. Thus he enables ghosts of

the dead to return to life or himself performs their terrible behest—visiting upon living men and women the iniquities they have committed against those now dead, and by this means bringing peace and rest to the souls of the latter which would else be travelling and troubling for ever."

From the numerous stories given by Mr. Watters in illustration of the popular belief in the fox's powers of transformation, I take only the following :—" It is as a pretty girl that the fox appears most frequently and does most mischief. Disguised as a woman it is always young and handsome, generally wicked, but on rare occasions very good. At times it puts on the garb and appearance of some one well known, but who is either dead or at a great distance. An accomplished scholar who resides in a village about twenty miles from Foochow told me not long ago a story which affords an illustration of this personation of particular individuals. A friend of his had ill-treated and, as was supposed, secretly killed a pretty young wife and married another. Soon after this latter event the house was reported to be haunted and no servant would remain in the family. The first wife's apartments were the worst of all, and this part of the premises had to be abandoned. Now one day my friend was reading with the master of the house in the works of Chuhsi, and they came to the passage which treats of ghosts and spirits. They then ceased reading and entered into a conversation on the subject, and the story of the haunted chambers was related. My friend laughed at and reproached the weakness which made a scholar believe in ghosts, and finally the two agreed to remove to that portion of the dreadful rooms. Before they had been seated here a long time, strange sounds became audible and soon the pit-pat of a woman's steps was heard. The door opened without any noise, and in walked the murdered woman clothed as of old. The blood forsook the two men's faces, speech fled their lips, and had it not been for the law of gravity their pigtails would have stood on end. There they sat paralyzed with mute awe and gazing on the spectre, which went pit-pat over the boards looking neither to right nor left until it reached the corner in which was a small wash-hand-stand with a basin of water. She took the basin in her hand and walked steadily with it over to the man who had been her husband, presenting it to him, when he instantly uttered a terrible scream and fell backwards. Then the spectral woman walked away and her patter was heard along the boards until she reached the outer door. My friend summoned up courage to go out and make investigation, but no human creature had been stirring, and only the fox which came almost daily had been seen on the premises. The house has been abandoned, the owner has gone elsewhere, but my friend believes that the ghost of the murderer's wife will torment him by means of a fox daily until it brings him to the grave."

It would be easy to multiply stories of this nature. I have three or four now before me not given by Mr. Watters, but their narration would unduly swell the limits of the chapter, while those who are curious on the subject can easily refer to Mr Watters's paper. I prefer therefore to turn to the analogies with Chinese belief presented elsewhere. Neither amongst the Semitic nor Aryan races can I find, in the authorities at my command, that any demoniacal power has ever been attributed to the fox. No reference to the animal appears in Brand, and in Continental Europe the wolf alone figures in fairy tales as the dangerous and crafty enemy of man. But we learn on the authority of Dr. Macgowan that " when the Pilgrim Fathers landed in Massachussets, they found the Indians, especially those of Naragannset, deeply imbued with fox superstitions, many of them similar to those mentioned above. Notices of these are found at considerable length in the works of the Rev. Mr. Elliot, known as the "Apostle of the Indians." In Japan, again, we find fox-myths a mighty power in the State Dr. Macgowan describes a primer the first book put into the hands of Japanese children; it was, profusely illustrated with wood-cuts, in which was depicted in full detail the progress of the Fox's courtship. First he was represented as a scholar learning his task, then he was a bachelor student in a state of meditation. Then a new scene opened with a couple of young lady foxes— the student's innamorata and her attendant; and so it went on through various stages of courtship, with its match-makers and middlemen, till the curtain fell on marriage, with its presents and trousseaux, and "living happy ever after." Thus, even in the education of childhood, the fox-myth weaves itself into the texture of Japanese thought. The fox was understood to be most mischievously inclined, and was especially mischievous in its domestic relations. It was believed, in Japan, to be no uncommon incident for a fox to transform itself into a charming young woman, who got married to some loving Japanese swain and had a family. By-and-bye something went awry in the domestic experiences, on which the mischievous fox-elf resumed her foxhood, and all her progeny did the same, and scampered off to their homes in dead men's tombs, leaving the late happy husband and father desolate and wretched." A recent newspaper paragraph, by the way, describes a murder committed at Chikuzen in which the murderer was discovered to be insane. Different members of his family, for three generations back, had gone mad, it was said, in consequence of one of their ancestors having injured a fox!—So much for the fox, thus summarily dismissed inasmuch as other writers have dealt so fully with his alleged powers.

Leaving the animal, for the mineral, world we note that even stones possess the reputation of being inhabited by spirits. A well-known Taoist legend relates that Chang Liang, a counsellor of the founder of the Han dynasty, derived his knowledge from a sage who was eventually metamorphosed into a yellow stone. Another legend tells how one of the immortals kept a flock of sheep who were changed to stone, but reassumed their proper shape at a word from their shepherd. A popular superstition recounts that in L'ien-chow, in the province of Kwang-si, when any person walking, happens to hit his foot against a stone, and afterwards gets

sick, his family immediately prepares an offering of fruit, wine, rice and incense; and proceeding to the spot, bow down and worship, after which the person gets well. They imagine that the stone is possessed by a demon. Gamblers frequently pray to stones thus possessed for "luck."

N. B. Dennys.

(To be continued.)

PAO-SZE:* THE CLEOPATRA OF CHINA.

A STORY OF THE SEVENTH CENTURY B.C.

(Continued from page 114.)

Soon after the Marquis of Shen had despatched his letter of remonstrance to King Yu, his messenger, who had been awaiting intelligence at the capital, on hearing that Kuo Shih-fu had been appointed to the command of an expedition to start at once to attack Shen, set off with all speed to inform the Marquis.

This intelligence threw him into a state of great alarm. "The country is small," he exclaimed, "and the army weak; how is it possible to oppose the hosts of the King?" A counsellor, Lü-tsao by name, approaching him, said, "The unrighteous conduct of the Son of Heaven, in divorcing the Queen in favour of a concubine, and elevating her son to the rank of heir-apparent, has caused every honest man to desert the throne; the King's action is generally condemned by the people; he stands unsupported in his power. Now as the army of the Si Jung, or western hordes (supposed to be the Turfans), is as powerful as that of Shen, I would suggest that a despatch be immediately sent to the Chief of the Jungs, soliciting the aid of troops, to go to the capital to save the Queen, and compel the King to confer the succession

on the legitimate crown prince, for such is the inheritance of the Chows."

The Marquis, considering the idea quite feasible, loaded a chariot with gold and silks, and despatched an envoy to the Chief of the Jungs, to ask for the aid of troops, promising at the same time that if he succeeded in capturing Kuo, he would allow him all the gold and wealth found in the treasuries. The Jung chief replied, "That as the King of China had lost the government of the country, he was quite willing, in response to the application of the Queen's father, to lend his aid in punishing the King's unprincipled conduct and re-instating the Queen," and simultaneously despatched an army of 15,000 men, in three divisions; the right under Po-ting, the left under Man Yay-suh, and the main or centre division under his personal command.

So great was the multitude that their weapons blocked the road, and their flags and banners obscured all space. The Marquis also marshalled his troops to render aid, and like an overwhelming torrent they marched to the attack of the capital, which they surprised, and so completely surrounded in lines three deep, that water could not have found a passage through them.

* Pao-sze was incorrectly printed Pao-sye in the first article.

As soon as King Yu heard the tumult that was going on outside, he was greatly alarmed. "Secrecy has not been observed," he exclaimed, "for here we are threatened with danger, and the Jung hordes are already upon us before our troops are marshalled. What is to be done?" Kuo Shih-fu replied, "Despatch men with all speed to light the alarm beacons, and succour is sure to come from the feudatory princes; and, by a combined attack from within and without, victory is sure to be ours." The King followed his counsel and sent men to light the beacons, but not a soldier responded to the summons, for the very good reason, as the reader will recollect, that when last the beacons were lit, it was to make dupes of the vassal princes, who now naturally thought that the signal was again a hoax, and not a soldier would they raise.

King Yu, seeing no succour was at hand and that the Jung hounds were besieging the city night and day, said to Kuo Shih-fu, "After all we do not know the strength of the Jung troops. Sally out and give them battle, meanwhile I will select and review our most valorous men, and lead them to action after you." Kuo Shih-fu was far from being a skilled general, but he could only reluctantly obey, so, taking two hundred chariots with him, he sallied out of the city gates, and marched to the attack.

The Marquis of Shen, who was at the head of his men arrayed in order of battle, on seeing Kuo Shih-fu emerging from the city, immediately pointed him out to the Jung chief, saying, "There is the base deceiver of the King and destroyer of the empire. Don't let him escape!" "Who'll go and capture him for me?" shouted the chief. "Your servant will go," answered Po-ting; and flourishing his sword and whipping his horse, he dashed straight at Kuo, who, after the exchange of less than ten blows, was felled from his chariot by a thrust from Po-ting's sword.

The Jung chief and Man Yay-suh now marched their troops together, and with loud huzzahs urged them on to the attack of the capital, which they entered, committing frightful slaughter on all sides. To every house they came across they applied the torch, and every person they met they put to the sword. Even the Marquis was quite powerless to restrain their fury, so they were left to plunder at will. Frightful disorder reigned in the city.

King Yu, who had not yet mustered his men, seeing the discomfiture of his first force, got a small cart, and putting Pao-sze and Pih-fu into it, made his escape through the private gate of the palace. The Minister of education, Earl Yu of Chêng (Chêng-pih yu), soon overtook him. "Sire!" he said, "have no fear, I will protect you," and conducting him out of the north gate, led him by a circuitous road to Mount Li. About half way there, they met Yin-ch'iu, who told them that the Jung troops had set fire to the palace, and were sacking the treasury; and that Chai Kung had been killed in the tumult. King Yu was quite harrowed with fright at this news.

Earl Yu of Chêng tried the beacons once more, but, although the smoke ascended to the skies, no help came.

The Jung troops now pursued them to the foot of Mount Li, and surrounded the palace, shouting "Don't let the dissolute King escape." As to the King, he and his favourite were sitting huddled together in a heap, wailing piteously. Earl Yu entering, aroused them. "There is no time to lose," he exclaimed, excitedly, "I am willing to sacrifice my poor life in assisting you to force through the crowd and flee to my state, where plans can be arranged for the recapture of the capital. "My obstinacy, O uncle," (the King called him uncle because Earl Yu of Chêng was brother to the late King Hsüan,) "in not following your counsel has brought about all this disorder. I will now place my life and that of my wife and child in your hands."

To mislead the Jungs, Earl Yu gave orders to his men to set fire to the Li palace, while he personally conducted the King through the crowd. With a spear which he carried he managed to open a way for himself, while Yin Ch'iu followed close behind with Pao-sze and her child under his care. They had not gone very far, when they were stopped by a lot of Jung soldiers under the command of an officer named Ku Li-chih. Earl Yu gnashed his teeth with rage at this opposition, but halted and gave him battle, and after a brief conflict felled him from his horse with a thrust from his spear. The Jung soldiers, seeing such bravery on the part of the Earl, were scattered for a time in dismay, but before he had gone half-a-mile their shouts recommenced, and Po-ting was seen coming in hot pursuit: "Go on in front and guard the king," Earl Yu said to Yin Ch'iu, "while I protect the rear;" which he did, fighting and following his charge alternately. The Jungs, however, managed to cut him off, and surround him; but although completely encompassed by these hounds, he lost none of his courage, and used his spear with superhuman dexterity. Any soldier foolhardy enough to come within reach met his death. The Jung chief now gave orders for a volley of arrows to be fired from all sides. Arrows fell like rain, and being no discriminators of persons, (*lit.* not distinguishing jade from stone,) the worthy minister of an unworthy King fell pierced by a myriad arrows. The left division under Man Yay-suh soon overtook the King's carriage and captured it.

The Jung chief, seeing the gorgeous dress and jade girdle of the occupant, knew it must be the King, so drawing up alongside the carriage he stabbed him with his sword, and then killed the prince. Pao-sze he spared on account of her rare beauty, and transferring her to a light travelling carriage, took her to his tent where he kept her for his own enjoyment. Yin Ch'iu hid himself in the boot of the carriage, but he was soon discovered and dragged out by the Jung soldiery, who summarily beheaded him.

Thus terminated the career of King Yu,

after a reign of ten years. His misfortunes may all be attributed to the unlucky rescue, by the husband of the vendor of *Yu* bows and *Ki* quivers, of that bewitching girl who possessed his mind, persecuted his wife, and now completed the ruin of the monarch and his country. How truly has the street children's song we quoted been fulfilled, and the prognostic that the years of his reign were numbered been confirmed!

Of a naturally dissolute, unprincipled and self-indulgent character, King Yu was quite unable to withstand the fascinations of this Chinese Cleopatra, who, like her ambitious prototype, reduced him by her evil influence to the state of an indolent voluptuary and submissive lover, in order that she might carry out her magnificent scheme of seeing her own offspring on the throne.

The Marquis of Shen, who had been all this time in the city, on seeing the palace in flames, hastened with all his men to extinguish them. After releasing the Queen from her "cold palace," he searched about the jewelled chamber for the King and Pao-sze, but not a trace could he find of them. A man, pointing to the north gate, told him they had gone out of it. He hurried off to overtake them, but on his way he met the Jung chief, returning with his cavalry and chariots. Mutual enquiries were exchanged as to their fortunes of war, when he learned that the King had been killed. This news caused the Marquis much grief and alarm. "My original idea," he said, "was merely to turn the King from his evil courses and to reinstate the Queen. Little did I think it would end like this. Hereafter in any case of disloyalty to the sovereign, posterity will cite me as an example." He then gave orders for the body of the King to be recovered and interred with royal honors. The Jung chief laughed in scorn at the sympathy shown by the Marquis, which he termed old woman's benevolence.

After the obsequies, the Marquis returned to the capital, where he gave a grand feast for the entertainment of the Jung chief;

and as the treasuries had already been emptied he loaded ten chariots with gold and silks to recompense him, hoping that this liberal reward would induce the chieftain to leave the city.

But who would have thought that the Jung chief would have considered the slaughter of the King an act which no amount of money could recompense, and, instead of evacuating the city, have taken up his abode in it, and spent the live-long day in revelry and debauchery, the thought of returning to his country never for a moment seeming to strike him?

The populace now began to murmur against the Marquis, and as he was quite helpless to act alone, he secretly addressed three despatches to the vassal princes of the neighbouring circuit, soliciting their preconcerted aid in support of the monarchy. The vassals addressed were Prince Ki-chow of Ch'in on the north, Prince Ki-ho of Wei on the east, and Yang-kai, the ruler of Tsin on the west; he further despatched a messenger to the state of Chéng, to announce the death of Earl Yu of Chéng to his son, the hereditary heir Wô-tô, at the same time instructing him to levy troops to avenge the death of his father. But of this, more anon. The hereditary heir, Wô-tô, was only just 23 years of age, but of immense stature and indomitable courage. On hearing of the death of his father in battle, his grief and ire were quite unconquerable. Without more ado, he dressed himself in mourning, and placed himself at the head of 300 chariots, which he led by forced marches to the rescue of the capital. Mounted scouts had, however, reported his approach to the Jung chief, who was quite prepared to receive him. On his arrival before the city Wô-tô, in his eager excitement, wanted to engage the enemy at once, but Kung Tze-chêng, his counsellor, remonstrated with him, telling him that the troops were too fatigued after their forced marches to commence the attack, and that it would be better to entrench themselves and quietly await the arrival of

the armies of the vassal princes, when a combined attack could be arranged which would ensure success. The impetuous Wô-tô could not be dissuaded. "In avenging the death of a father," he said, "the rites admit of no procrastination or looking back. Moreover, the traitorous Jungs, gloating over their success, will be unprepared for attack: we have only to advance to conquer; but if we wait for the arrival of the allies, the ardour and fire of our troops will have died out;" so, urging his men on, he drove his chariot right up to the city wall.

The banners on the battlements were toppling about in disorder, and not a drum was heard, nor a sign of activity visible. Wô-tô, railing at them from beneath the wall, challenged them to fight. "Ye beasts of robbers," he said, "why don't you come out and exterminate the enemy?" No response came from the walls. Wô-tô therefore gave orders to commence the assault on the city.

Suddenly the sound of trumpets was heard in a wood outside the city, and simultaneously a body of troops was seen emerging from behind the thickets, advancing to the attack. Wô-tô was thrown into a state of great alarm, but he lost no time in bringing his spearmen into line to receive them. Trumpets were now heard on the wall, and the gates being thrown open, another detachment came out to join in the attack. With Po-ting in front and Man Yay-suh in rear, attacking simultaneously, Wô-tô was overpowered, and being utterly routed, beat a hasty retreat, the Jung troops pursuing him for over ten miles. Such was the Jung chief's plan to engage his enemy. After Wô-tô had collected his scattered army, he confessed to his counsellor Kung Tze-chêng, that he had lost his chance by his refusal to listen to his advice, and further asked what they should do, and where they should go. Tze-chêng advised, that as Po-yang, the capital of Wei, was not far distant, they should go there and seek the co-operation of the Prince of Wei, a very trustworthy and experienced man, and with the combined forces of Wei and Chêng they might accomplish their task.

Wô-tô agreed to this suggestion, and his troops were turned towards Po-yang. They had scarcely marched two days, when they perceived a dense cloud of dust in the horizon, and presently innumerable horses and chariots appeared advancing like a wall before them. In their midst sat a prince, dressed in embroidered robes and golden girdle. He was of dark complexion, with grey hair, of elegant carriage, and possessing quite the air of one of the genii. This person was no other than prince Ki-ho of Wei, a man of 80 winters, and the very person they were going to seek. Wô-tô halted his chariot, and addressing him in a loud voice said, "I am Wô-tô, the hereditary heir of Chêng. The Jung hounds have rebelled in the capital against the royal troops, and my father has been killed on the field of battle. I, too, have suffered a defeat, and am therefore come expressly to seek your highness' aid." The prince bowed and replied, "Pray let the hereditary heir of Chêng ease his mind. I and my people are loyal to the crown. Furthermore, I hear the armies of Ch'in and Tsin are close at hand, and will shortly be here. Verily the Jungs may now be pitied."

Wô-tô at once resigned the vanguard to the prince of Wei, and both armies marched towards the capital, Kuo.

When within seven miles they diverged in different directions, and encamped behind stockades. Scouts were sent out to ascertain the whereabouts of the Ch'in and Tsin armies, and in a very short time one returned with the news that towards the western horizon the sound of horns and the rumbling of wheels might be heard, and that he had seen the banners bearing the character Ch'in (秦) in large letters. "Though only a barony," remarked the Prince of Wei, "these Ch'ins are well accustomed to fighting the Jungs, and being fond of warfare and of a daring nature, are much feared

by the western hordes." He had scarcely finished speaking when the spy from the north returned to report that the Tsin army had arrived, and had already encamped behind stockades off the north gate. The Prince of Wei was much pleased at this news, and exclaimed exultingly, "Now that the armies of the two states have arrived our noble mission will be accomplished." A messenger was sent to the camps with friendly enquiries to the rulers of Ch'in and Tsin, and shortly after, the two chieftains found themselves in the camp of the Prince of Wei, talking over the mutual trials of the campaign. The mourning worn by Wô-tô attracted the attention of the two chieftains, who enquired who he was. The Prince of Wei informed them he was the heir of Chêng, and gave them an account of the death of his father, Earl Chêng, and of the murder of the King, which failed not to elicit their profound sympathy.

"May I ask what plan of attack you have in view," said the Prince of Wei, addressing the two chieftains, "for I am too old and inexperienced to be of much use, but as a servant of the King I could not refrain from coming to give assistance; I however, rely on you completely to exterminate these pests."

"As the Jungs only fight for rapine and plunder," replied the Ch'in chief, "they are sure to be feasting and revelling, and doubtless think that as our armies have only just arrived we shall be unprepared to attack; I propose the city should be assaulted from three sides, north, south, and east, leaving the west gate as a sole means of exit, outside which, at some distance off, let Wô-tô and his men be stationed to cut off their retreat, thus ensuring a complete victory." The Prince of Wei declared the plan an admirable one, but of this more hereafter.

The Marquis of Shen, who was still inside the city, on hearing of the arrival of the troops sent by the vassal princes, was greatly rejoiced. He at once entered into a secret plot with Chai Kung's son, Huan, to surrender the gates. Meanwhile he urged the Jung chief to get his spoil out of the city, and advised that Po-ting be sent with a strong detachment from the right division to escort the booty back to his state, by which means he hoped to reduce his forces. Man Yay-suh was directed to take his entire division outside the city to meet the enemy, the Marquis' scheme being to separate their forces as much as possible; and the Jung chief, acting in good faith, and not suspecting treachery, followed out the programme entirely.

Man Yay-suh had encamped right opposite Prince Wei's earthworks. The arrangement was that the assault was not to commence till early the next morning, but the excited troops of Wei commenced the attack about midnight and carried the stockades by storm. Man Yay-suh, grasping his sword and mounting his horse, hastened to meet the enemy, but as the Jung soldiers had scattered in dismay, he also fled with his army, as his two fists and single pair of arms were powerless to oppose the enemy. The allies, from the other side, now ordered the attack on the city to commence, when suddenly the gates were thrown open, and the combined armies marched in without opposition. The Jung chief, who was in the midst of his dreams, awoke in a state of fright, and seizing a bare-backed horse, mounted it, and escaped with a few hundred followers by the west gate. The heir of Chêng, Wô-tô, engaged him in battle, and his position was becoming very critical, when Man Yay-suh, who had managed to collect some of his scattered troops together, came

to the rescue, and eventually succeeded in saving his chief. Wô-tô would not venture to pursue him, but entered the city, and met the allied chiefs, by which time it was broad daylight.

Pao-sze, whom the author has left unnoticed all this time, being unable to follow her captor, strangled herself.

Thus perished the beautiful favourite of Yu Wang, the Dark King. The evil influence exercised by this voluptuous beauty over the King appears to have completely paralyzed a nature already quite incapable of any vigorous action. Her power seems to have rested in her actual beauty, and, unlike her Egyptian compeer, it is evident that she was not gifted with any mental qualities beyond those displayed in the furtherance of her schemes and intrigues; for, as the poet has said in special allusion to her and her creatures,

"Those from whom come no lesson, no instruction,
Are women and eunuchs."

And as most of the disorders recorded in ancient history are traceable to the intrigues and follies of woman, the sentiment expressed above is generally accepted as correct. "Only a Chinaman however, will agree that it is a bad thing for a woman to be wise. The writer of the ode seems to have thought that there was something inherently, essentially, vicious in female nature, so that what were virtues in a man, and instruments of good, became, when possessed by a woman, transmuted into vices and instruments of evil."

H. KOPSCH.

AN INTRODUCTION TO A RETROSPECT OF FORTY YEARS OF FOREIGN INTERCOURSE WITH CHINA,

AND

A REVIEW OF HER RELATIONS WITH JAPAN.*

(Continued from page 199.)

Reluctantly expressing these misgivings, I intend no disparagement of the actual progress attained in Japan; but, on the contrary, hail the marks of it with self-elation, as the legitimate results of the tentative and conciliatory policy so auspiciously inaugurated by the estimable Commodore Perry† and since so wisely persevered in by his successors in the continuous effort to win that estranged sister to the comity of Nations;— Sir Harry Parkes being conspicuous in this by reason of repeated exigencies during his lengthy term of office there.

I applauded the initiatory achievement of the lamented Perry in a farewell address that was unanimously accepted by the American community at Canton; and as it has become a part of the historical record of that period, of twenty years ago, and is in its tenor not only illustrative of my present meaning, but forms in itself a distinct mark of the initial point of a new epoch,—that of the induction of Japan into the sisterhood of civilized Nations,—I reproduce it here.

We are all prone, perhaps, to magnify or idealize our heroes; but to-day the voice of the world echoes my appreciation of his deserts, and Japan especially owes a debt of gratitude to his memory.

The address is dated "Canton, September 4th, 1854," and I quote from a printed copy of that period.

" CANTON, *September 4th*, 1854.
" *His Excellency Commodore* MATTHEW C. PERRY, *Commander-in-Chief of the Naval Forces of the United States in East India, China and Japan Seas, and late Special Envoy to Japan, &c., &c.*

" Sir,—We, your countrymen, the undersigned Merchants and residents in China, learning that it is Your Excellency's intention to leave for the United States on the 11th current, desire to declare to you before your departure, the sense we entertain of your services in fulfilment of the mission with which you were specially charged by our Government to that of Japan, and to acknowledge the promptitude with which you have bestowed the protection so much required by the important interests at stake in this country and its neighborhood during your command in these seas.

" Enjoying the advantages of proximity, and with our interest heightened thereby, it has been our privilege twice to witness your departure for the shores of Japan, nor will you have doubted that you went with our best wishes freighted; participating, indeed, in the hopes and anxieties attending your great enterprise, in perhaps a greater degree than those who were more distant, we may, as your countrymen, now claim the right to anticipate the warm approval—the pride and satisfaction—with which the announcement of your achievements will be hailed in our common country.

" But your success, which is so well calculated to enkindle the patriotism and awaken the admiration and gratitude of your countrymen, will not in a less degree elicit the applause of other nations.

* A lecture delivered at Concordia Hall, Canton, December 8th, 1874.
† Commodore being then the highest title allowed by Congress to the Navy.

" You cannot have been unconscious that your audience was the whole civilized world; and that your mission was worthy of man's highest ambition; whilst this added to your anxieties, it has not lessened your zeal or dazzled your mind; but has called into exercise that rare assemblage of qualities—that union of conciliation with firmness, the happy tact and judgment—which have ensured your complete success.

" That such will be the award of your own countrymen and of the people of other nations, we hazard nothing in declaring.

" Whilst you have thus elevated yourself to a proud position in the eyes of the world, you have firmly reëstablished the hold which the name you bear has so long had upon the hearts of your countrymen; and the name of Perry, which has so long adorned the naval profession, will henceforth be enrolled with the highest in diplomacy:—Columbus, De Gama, Cook, La Pérouse, Magellan,—these inscribed their names in history by striving with the obstacles of nature; you have conquered the obstinate will of man, and, by overturning the cherished policy of an empire, have brought an estranged but cultivated people into the family of nations. You have done this without violence; and the world has looked on with admiration, to see the barriers of prejudice fall before the flag of our country without the firing of a shot.

" It is thus that your acts, dictated by your wisdom and inspired by your justice and benevolence, have so auspiciously inaugurated the entrance of Japan into the great family of nations, the consequences of which affect the welfare of the universe; and thus that, in adding lustre to the flag of our country, you have durably inscribed your name upon the history of the world.

" In conclusion, permit us to say that, as none of your countrymen can more fully appreciate the value of your services, so none will more sincerely desire to hear of your future welfare; and to request your acceptance of a durable Memorial of your visits to China, as a testimony of the estimation in which we hold your public services and private character.

" Wishing you the highest reward that man can bestow—that of a whole nation's gratitude,

We remain, Sir, your countrymen,

Signed by all the American Merchants in Canton.

It is somewhat singular that it was just another decade when the next marked event in the foreign annals of Japan occurred, as recorded in a circular sent my friends, dated " Canton, 23rd September, 1864."

CANTON, *23rd September*, 1864.

" We now have not only the satisfaction of advising a continued ameliorative tendency in political affairs in China; but a decidedly progressive step in the same direction in Japan, as the result of the coöperative coercive pressure recently applied by the Foreign Powers ostensibly against an individual Prince—Nagato—who, however, in acknowledging the lapse from Treaty obligations and promising amity in future, declares the complicity of the Rulers of the Country generally in the obstructive measures taken by him at the entrance to the Inland Sea.

Whether as participators or merely passive observers, the complete military success of this conjoint movement of the British, French, Netherlands and American forces, superadded to the moral effect of the previously established diplomatic accord of those Powers, has so impressed the Rulers of the Country that we may safely assume a better understanding in future: And, indeed, the reluctance evinced by the Foreign Powers to any act of apparent hostility and the deliberation with which they arrived at unanimity and proceeded to actual—though circumscribed and local - coercion, partakes more of the tentative than the dominating or dictatorial policy;—so that we may acquiesce in and welcome these results as well deserved, whatever repugnance we may feel to the application of force in general in that Country."

It is the triumph of this firm, though tentative and conciliatory policy that we behold in Japan to-day. The actual progress as I regard it, however, is little deeper than the political conversion of the Rulers. That was necessarily the first step in the actual condition of the country; and I acknowledge that the fruit is golden, though the harvest seems ended for the present. I say seems to be, because in our impatience we grudge acknowledgement of the progress that is continuous.

Such is the fruit of the application by the Western powers to Japan, after lamentable aberrations and miscarriages in relations with China, of the deep wisdom of one of the most venerated Sages of the latter country—Mencius,—embodied in the following words:—" *He who subdues men by force is a tyrant; he who subdues them by philanthropy is a King; Those who subdue by force do not subdue the heart; but those who subdue men by virtue gain the hearts of the subdued and their submission is sincere.*"

In further considering the effects of the two differing politics of China and Japan—that is, " judging the tree by its fruit,"—we are struck with the remarkable contrast presented by the prime test of vigor and prosperity in a race or nation, that, namely, of increase of population.

We find that notwithstanding the exemption of Japan from Foreign war and serious or protracted civil commotion for several centuries, its growth of population has been very slow; whereas China, notwithstanding the wars with tributary States and Foreign powers and its still more destructive rebellions, shews a vast increase of population in the same period.

From this we may deduce a much greater fecundity as the distinguishing characteristic of its people; and this, in turn, we must attribute to its superior domestic polity as derived from the wisdom of its ancient Rulers and wise men. The maxims of the Sages governing the relations of the sexes in family life affect the preservation and duration of the race, and hence the vital prosperity of the Empire; and evince a prescient wisdom that Japan, and some Western Nations also, might well profit by. The imperative maxim that every man should so conduct himself as to have sons of his own, and thus assure the preservation and increase of families, lies at the root of the duration of family and national life; as does the rule that no man can marry a woman of the same clan or surname. Thus it is that sons are cherished and reared with care, and a suitable mate sought for each by the parents, at an early age. And so important has marriage been regarded by the ancient worthies that objection was taken to the Buddhist religion because the celibacy of its priests would constitute a dangerous innovation.

In this idea the Chinese do but conform to the general idea of the ancient world, when celibacy was regarded with great disfavor.

Pursuing the contrast further, as presented by the respective idiosyncracies of the two peoples, we see in the Japanese a readiness of affront and proneness to war, the very opposite of the temperament of the Chinese; and we recognize this at once as the fruit of the feudal system, with its favored military caste:—"As the twig is bent the tree's inclined" never had more pointed illustration in a national trait than this

affords; nor was ever contrast more marked between neighboring nations.

So it is that, on the other hand, we may declare of the Chinese people as emphatically that their genius is not for war; a trait their conquerors might well approve. And so fully have they done so, that we may also say of them, that they have become less prone to war themselves, and, in turn, are being morally conquered by the arts of peace.

Hence, distinction is won by literary proficiency more readily than by military achievement: Rewards for the former are permanently incorporated in the system of Government; whereas those for the latter depend wholly upon the Emperor's special recognition. And so, also, as a learned student* has told us in his instructive and graceful notes upon Chinese poetry, and exemplified by translations from it, it is by literary excellence and especially by poetical accomplishments that, in the ideal of the highest ranks of life, at least, lovers win a mistress; that not by deeds of chivalry, but by piercing the heart of the fair one with a poetic arrow, can the heart's blood be drawn.

Thus it is that literary honors are the prime incentives to ambitious youth.

Is it the influence of this predominance given to literary culture for so many ages, that accounts for the absence of the chivalrous in their dispositions and of that twin trait, a nice sense of personal honor, the ever vigilant *amour propre* that cultured Europeans have, and that is also exhibited by the Japanese; and the want of which quality seems the more striking because of their excessive punctilio in forms of personal intercourse?

Is it not, rather, to be found in their natural coldness and want of heart, for whose origin we must look even further back, whereat also lies the germ of the degradation of woman and the cruelty to daughters especially?

These are distinguishing features of their civilization of great interest in estimating

* Mr. Gardner.

the probabilities of radical changes, I had almost said *possibilites* of change, in considering the intricacy and indissoluble nature of such a condition of society. Civilization is the fruit of the application of the faculties of the mind and heart in their greater intensity to the affairs of life; and it is in the direction of these faculties that the practical bent of a race is determined.

The teachings of China's most venerated Sages are undeniably largely in consonance with the principles of a high morality and of that "peace and good will to man" which a later and incomparable Teacher inculcated in the West; but they are wholly lacking in the humility that He taught as proper to all men. They were animated by a spirit of exclusiveness and assumed benevolence toward other races of men, derived from the ascription of divine attributes to their Emperors; which is of the very root of all idolatry,[*] that like the deadly upas spreads wide its treacherous shade, absorbing the vital principle of life in the body politic.

True, one of them, Meh-tsi, taught universal love and benevolence, in contradistinction to the selfish code of Confucius; but he was discarded after the violent onslaughts of Mencius against him. Obviously Meh-tsi had glimmerings of the healing rays destined to converge upon the West some centuries later.

The figure of the most renowned of those Sages is presented by a great English poet of the last century as superlatively grand, in contradistinction to other moral philosophers, when—

" Superior and alone Confucius stood,
　　Who taught that useful science—to be
　　good."

Yes, as the poet phrases, "*to be good*." But as one of the Stoics, not as a Christian; nor even as one instinct of the integrity and warmth of Nature; for Confucius taught from the selfish point of view, whereat love

[*] It is true that to a great extent this is now but an antiquated sentiment.

of one's enemies was not discernible as a principle of life: And his teaching utterly lacks the vital element of human sympathy; that divine element that the Savior brought us as the only sure bond of peace, when He said, "Bear ye one another's burdens."

And we may here notice the contrast that has been so eloquently drawn by Guizot between the essentially humanizing influences of Christianity and the stoical inertness of Paganism. "It is to the honor of Christian civilization that it has carried repentance into the souls of nations: England has repented of having oppressed Ireland; Europe has repented of having practised Slavery;"—(and I may now add, America has repented of Slavery in blood and ashes!) —"Pagan antiquity knew nothing of these awakenings of the public conscience, of these moral illuminations which suddenly change the hearts of men, and ere long effect a corresponding change in the state of societies."

But as to the general results of the inculcations of the Sages of China, whatever the lapses may meantime have been, we find existing, among other indices of civilization, the facts: first, the general diffusion of education among the population—exclusive of females generally, however; and that the proportion of the community exclusively devoted to letters is much greater than in any other country. Secondly, That of the recognition of the individual in his rights as a man and his equality before the Law;— that is, under the Penal Code as the law of the land, to which the Emperor himself is amenable: This responsibility of the Emperor to the people not being deemed inconsistent with the fundamental, but somewhat sentimental, principle of the polity of China of filial piety constraining veneration of him as the Father of the people.

Whatever the measure of influence of this teaching of their Sages upon individual character may be, or whatever the aggregate effect in certain respects, if we take a broader view of the polity of this ancient people, and consider that "the civilizing rule requires the greatest possible use of the moral agencies only," we must acknowledge that China's reluctance to War evinces high civilization.

And we may here pause at the reflection that their retrogressive steps toward a return to the barbaric instinct for War, are taken under modern incitements and foreign instruction: Nor can we escape the mortification of acknowledging, at the same time, as a proof of our inconsistency, that the higher mind of our own countries recognizes the truth of the declaration of the first President of the French Association for the advancement of Science, that "the strength and glory of a Country are not in its Arms, but in its Science."

It is curious to observe in the attribution of faculties of an omniscient character to gifted scholars by the Chinese,—who consider a Mandarin of literary eminence capable of conducting a military campaign,—a parallel of the days of Homer;—whose devotees regarded him as a master of strategy, medicine, music, and other arts which he has commemorated; and even thought themselves qualified, by their proficiency in his writings, to assume the command of an army at any moment.

Historians tell us that among the ancient Egyptians intelligence and scholastic culture were considered superior to or held in higher esteem than military prowess and material possessions; and it is interesting to note in this what is perhaps the most significant of the resemblances in the characteristics of the two peoples as indicative of a common origin.

But as to the ancient Greeks and Romans, we are told by the learned Dugald Stewart, that the proof of China's attainment of a higher point of civilization than they, was the invention of the art of printing and the manner of it:—"That the discovery was not accidental, but rather the result of those general causes on which the progress of society seems to depend, and in fact

marking a step in the social history of man." [*]

In these portraitures as exhibiting the natural traits of the Chinese, there may be marked a distinction from their conquerors, the Manchu Tartars, in that the latter have a more soldier-like frankness and less of the subtle deceit that is the offspring of a conscious weakness of character. In this the Manchu resembles the Japanese. Yet there are numerous instances of a heroic spirit among the Chinese, quite rivalling those signalizing the devoted valor of the Manchus. Such, for example, as that of Admiral Kwan, who at the battle of the Bocca Tigris—after his fleet had been destroyed in the offing,—resolutely landed and fought the British seamen hand to hand in the Anunghoy forts, where he fell; winning the highest admiration of his foes: who, upon the removal of his body, fired minute guns from the ship of the line "Blenheim." He rightly claimed to be a descendant from the God of War, Kwan-Tae, who was also a native of one of the northwestern provinces; and his brilliant emulation of his deified ancestor's renown furnishes a conspicuous example of hereditary genius.

However curious these resemblances or parallelisms or striking the contrasts with Japan, and however interesting the question of the common origin of some of the ancient peoples, the essential fact presented to-day is the numerical inadequacy and personal inefficiency of China's defensive forces,—produced under the system of training that we have thus reviewed,—to cope with European or even Japanese aggression. Which brings us to the consideration of the circumstances of the issue with Japan.

The contrasts to which I have adverted always presented elements of estrangement between the two Empires; but whether in

[*] Whatever weight we accord this opinion, we must be mindful that the special knowledge of the Greeks in several departments of Science and Art was superior to that of the Chinese. In Medical Science, for instance, it was emphatically so.

former times Japan could have maintained her independence of China under any other than the feudal and essentially military system, may well be doubted. It was her necessity then. Certainly it served the purpose of her relatively inconsiderable people to roll back the tide of all but universal conquest to which the Mongols aspired, and to inspire a respect for the valor of those capable of such achievements, that has continued to this day.

In considering the differing traits of the two peoples and the relative resources of the two Empires as incentives to war, we have to balance Japanese valor and military aptitude against Chinese sturdiness of character and greater material and numerical power.

The isolation of Japan for more than two centuries, presumably and avowedly in consequence of the intrigues of the Jesuit Missionaries, tended to prevent fresh collisions with China. There was a legacy of mutual hate at the end of the sixteenth century, from the old attempts at conquest by the Mongols; the retaliatory raids of the Japanese upon the Chinese coasts; and the wars undertaken by Taikosama in the Corea.

We thus reach the present moment, when we see the characteristic native pride of the Japanese inflated as against China by their greater acquirements and aptitude in European training. Yet in this imputation I do not intend to imply blame of their Government in respect to the origin of the question regarding aboriginal Formosa. On the contrary, I adhere to the view that I publicly stated in a letter of the 7th of August from Amoy (vide *China Mail* of the 11th idem); which, lest I may seem a blind partisan of China, I here reproduce:—

" Considering all the facts as presented from this advantageous point of view, although as yet without special knowledge of the real present purposes of the Government of Japan, I must declare my own opinion as justifying it in measures of a disciplinary character against aboriginal Formosa, whose independence of China has always been successfully maintained and not less practically acknowledged by China herself.

Apart from the fact that if not Japan herself, yet her dependency Loo Choo had a Colony, on the east coast of Formosa long prior to the acquirement of territorial rights by China on its West Coast, the Government of Japan is but applying the principles imposed upon itself by that of the United States in the Treaties of Commodore Perry and Hon. Townsend Harris. In opening up aboriginal Formosa by coercion, and in exacting compensation for performing the duties which contiguity alone might properly impose upon China, as a condition of the relinquishment of conquests thus righteously acquired, Japan cannot rightly be stigmatised as the party evincing a hostile spirit. On the other hand, the nations of Christendom may reproach themselves for a tardiness in dealing effectively with aboriginal Formosa, which has been fatal to many of their own citizens and the natives of all contiguous countries."

The movement ostensibly against aboriginal Formosa is regarded by the Chinese people, however, as aggressive toward the sovereignty of the west coast of the Island, so that its form forbids the sympathy of any party in China; and, on the other hand, arouses the *amour-propre* of the majority, binding them to the policy of the Government. We shall see in this case, therefore, what I have repeatedly remarked, that although appearances are suggestive of the fragility of the political entity—China—that its name implies and that a descending blow may scatter it in pieces, yet if the arm that deals it is a Foreign one: Behold how congruous become the scattered fragments of a ruin!—the Empire gains again in cohesion: Like a relic of fine old 'cracklin' porcelain, the seeming fragments closely adhere under the surface.

The controversy undeniably has an important bearing upon the general relations of the Western Nations with these two Eastern Empires and goes far to contradict the alleged declaration of Prince Bismarck at the Vienna Exposition, that "it will be time enough to occupy ourselves with the East in the twentieth century." It is a controversy that in its origin and continuance strikingly illustrates the differing Administrations of the two Governments. We see that of China in this, as in all similar matters of administration, governed by incidents and the slave of expediency:

whereas that of Japan is characterized by a firm policy and energetic initiative that overrules incidents by anticipating them.

The question is seriously complicated because China desires, on the one hand, to profit by imposing the restraints of international Law upon Japan, while, on the other, neglecting, herself, its correlative obligations. And it will only be by the constraining salutary influence of the judicious friends of the two Empires at Peking that a rupture, involving a protracted war, with all its inevitable train of disastrous consequences, will be averted.

Perhaps we have already derived the only unqualified benefit incident to an estrangement of the two Nations, in the obvious effect it has had to check the conservative reaction in China, as against the Western Powers;—for a war even of short duration between the two, would endanger their relations with each of the Western Powers and even portend wide-spread complications among the latter. Continued peace between China and Japan, on the other hand, may be regarded as promising a salutary influence, in that the adoption of Western ideas by Japan is an example for China to profit by, that open antagonism between the two would retard.

We are prone to find in the immediate circumstances the cause of controversy and the origin of hostilities; but to thus circumscribe our view in this case would be to ignore the latent springs of action, on the one side, and the laxity of system on the other;—whose respective origins lie far back in the training of the past. And in this we find the key to the halting, indecisive character of the negotiations at Peking on this question.

I have thus read what I wrote more than a month ago; and to-day I think you will agree with me that the actual course of the negotiations down to the eve of the application of the good offices of H E. Mr. Wade, —when those negotiations had ended in

utter failure,—had in no respect contradicted the sense of my words; but, rather, that the whole course of events has served to give point to the opinions I had expressed. The terms of the settlement, also, in the according of an indemnity to Japan, have justified the view taken in my letter of August 7th from Amoy;—whilst the contrarieties in the views taken of H. E. Mr. Wade's action, by the several publicists at the North and in Hongkong, illustrate the whole subject of foreign relations with the two Empires, and especially those with China, in a way to confirm the survey that I had taken of the difficulties in the way of any attempts to effect radical changes in China.

It is inevitable that such a question,—in the respective conditions and relative positions of the two powers and of their relations to the Western Nations,—should evoke a contrariety of opinions. The very intricacy of the subject as a whole precludes precision of thought; and we can concur only in a balancing of probabilities in regard to the solution of any question that may arise.

Some writers, in commenting upon the adjustment of this dispute, avow themselves the partisans of China, but in the sense of imposed reform of her Government: War on Japan is to be made righteous by its imputed regenerating effect upon China herself!—This is especially the point of an animated indictment of H. E. Mr. Wade, by a correspondent of the *N. C. Daily News*, just to hand, whose *nom de plume* is "Kin-ming." And the Editor of that Journal distinctly claims that H. E. rendered an essential service to China in healing the issue with Japan; urging, moreover, that he should have exacted a *quid pro quo* as a proof of the appreciation of China. From Japan we also just now hear of the special invitation given Sir Harry Parkes to an audience of the Sovereign, when His Majesty "expressed his warm appreciation of the eminent services rendered Japan by H. E. Mr. Wade."

China and Japan both benefitted,—who shall begrudge the assured reward ?

Notwithstanding some misgivings at the North, I think we may not only assume the adjustment as substantially completed, but count upon the influence of it as highly salutary.

I now resume the thread of the lecture as originally written.

However peaceful the adjustment of this Formosan question, we must, in future, look for the influence of Japan as a new feature in the field of diplomacy at Peking, with such complications as the Corean question or the Loo Chooan question may produce,—a new and essentially Eastern element added to the already somewhat complex problem engaging the attention of the diplomatists there.

But, whatever play this may give to the faculties of those astute and mysterious members of the Legations who, impatient of a seemingly sterile routine, crave an occasion to "flutter the Volseians," we may hope that it will not contribute to make Peking in any serious sense another Constantinople, an arena of diplomatic fencing of the most animated kind, such as we saw in the Turkish capital before 1854, when the 'Sick-man' there seemed tottering to his fall and held up by Britain, France and Austria, to keep, as we may call it, that *Sublime Porte* from the grasp of another Power; and where those trusty Ministers who represented the three Powers were wont to feel the Imperial pulse of Russia.

———

To resume, as to the regeneration of the Chinese people. The problem remains a gordian knot; and of greater coherence and intricacy the greater the external pressure becomes. We may recall the tradition of the original gordian knot, that he who should untie it should become Ruler of Asia; but we may well be warned against summoning another Alexander from without to cut this modern one, lest the charm be thereby broken and we fail to unravel the

mystery aright, or, recklessly cutting the knot, overwhelm ourselves in a flood of unutterable woes !

There was a time when a desperate remedy of the kind was the desiderated solution of accumulated and multiform evils, and no reproach could have attached to its application ; but that opportunity to right great wrongs was squandered : and having ourselves aided to rebind the people to their alien Rulers, it is becoming in us to participate in the consequence unmurmuringly; if, indeed, we cannot do so cheerfully, in the light of philosophically reconciling considerations.

From that time forward foreign pressure has been an element of great strength to the Government as against internal rebellious movements ; such as that of Ho Aluk against Canton in 1854, in sympathy with the Tae-ping Rebellion, when, although the most of the province was controlled by his party and the city itself beleagured for several months by his forces, Whampoa and the approaches even to the Fort in the Macao passage, on the South, and the White Cloud hills on the North, in their possession, yet the purses of the petted gentry kept the city walls intact and rolled the tide of revolution back from their crumbling buttresses.

We are prone to invoke philosophy in argument, yet reluctant to apply it practically, such is the intensity of our craving for early fruits.

Surely we need its influence if we would aid the Chinese people to grope their way from the labyrinth wherein their sages left them so long ago ; a labyrinth whose length and intricacy seem increased to their eyes by the obtrusive glare of our western effulgence.

A precipitate rupture from without would not aid them.

We must, therefore, cease to regard their statesmen with jaundiced eyes. We shall but stultify ourselves if we regard not with clear vision what their point of view must, in the nature of things, be. They stand behind the accumulated traditions and precedents of ages; and they are the recognized defenders of this bulwark of the ancient system, exercising their trust under the jealous eyes of a scrupulously reverent people.

In point of fact, the conservatives of China are not altogether unlike those of a certain country on the eastern side of the Atlantic, who, in the egotism that admits of nothing comparable to the old routine, sturdily oppose all influences from without and especially all assimilation to the ameliorative modes of life or Government which its children, invigorated by direct contact with the primeval forces of Nature, have engrafted upon the sturdy parent stock. The Chinese conservatives do but out-herod Herod; and it is one of the most curious of anomalies that they are accorded by the most progressive of peoples a measure of tolerance that the conservatives of England deny them.

It behoves us to remember that they are far short of a claim to statesmanship who fail to concede to all men their *amour propre;* and that if this is true of the Nations of Christendom, it is all the more incumbent upon us in dealing with the Rulers of a people of an ancient civilization, who are imbued with the philosophical spirit that we have noticed in Tseng-quo-fan and who are as yet but at the threshold of comity. And in our attitude toward the people themselves, we have need to be constantly mindful of the broad difference between the level of their modes of thought and our own.

If in contrasting the two systems of civilization and faith as furnishing incentives to action or restraint, we say broadly that the fundamental difference between us lies in the recognition or non-recognition of the principle of perfectibility, we shall not perhaps widely err:—That is to say, they are content with their garnered store of the wisdom of the ancients; laying to their souls the flattering unction that the standard in

moral and intellectual training, the *summum bonum* for themselves as a people, was reached ages ago; and that an outward conformity to dogma and formalism and an emulative proficiency in the classics, suffice for the perpetuation of the virtue and intelligence of the race.

Whereas, we, on the contrary, are instinct with the truth that the welfare and salvation of the race lies in striving ever, and with cumulative zeal. That progress is the stamp of life in Nations as in individuals. That not to advance is to recede; that decay is the doom of inanition. That the goal of human endeavor is perfectibility; that every step upward but reveals a higher round of the ladder whose top reaches to heaven. That this principle of life is the heritage of our faith. That in Europe we trace the assured advance of civilization from and with the spread of Christianity. From its initial point in the individual, advancing to the family; thence to the community; thence to the nation; and thence to the western world in general.

That the highest civilization is resultant of and inseparable from Christianity, whose distinguishing characteristic is human sympathy; the vital element that lies at the root of progressive social improvement. And thus that it is especially distinctive from Paganism in that moral growth is assured by inherent laws of vitality prescribing the alliance of physical, mental and moral excellence. That the assimilative desire, the longing for beauty and the admiration of moral excellence are in essence one and in their highest manifestations precursory of the craving for immortality; and hence constitute the vital procreative principle of a redeemed humanity;—whence we deduce the ultimate survival of the fittest and the approximation to that perfectibility to which we are summoned.

As a philosopher has said:—"The essence of the moral is change for the better: On the one hand we are children of the past;

on the other, fathers of the future." And as a poet more eloquently sings:—

"As Heaven and Earth are fairer, fairer far
Than Chaos and blank darkness, the once
    chiefs;
And as we show that beyond that Heaven
    and Earth
In form and shape compact and beautiful,
In will, in action free, companionship,
And thousand other signs of purer life,—
So on our heels a new perfection treads,
A power more strong in beauty, born of us
And fated to excel us, as we pass
In glory that old darkness."

Or, as sweet Edmond Spenser, in a still loftier strain, sang 300 years ago:—

"Beautie is not, as fond men misdeeme,
An outward show of things that only seeme.
  .   .   .   .
Vouchsafe, then, O Thou most Almightie
    Spright!
From whom all gifts of wit and knowledge
    flow,
To shed into my breast some sparkling light
Of thine Eternall Truth, that I may show
Some little beames to mortall eyes below
Of that immortall Beautie, there with Thee
Which in my weake distraughted mynd I
    see."

These gifted minds thus remind us of the ever interchangable alliance between the beautiful and the true. That the love of the beautiful is, therefore, the connecting link between the animal and spiritual in our nature, which can only be perfected to a harmoniously complete realization of our ideal by Christianity; that is to say, Christianity perfects a reconciliation that culture alone, as we see in the history of Grecian civilization, vainly tries to accomplish.

If these were but transcendental aspirations of our cherishing, they are such as the Chinese mind of the present day cannot conceive of. For theirs is a pedantic transcendentalism, whose horizon is limited to the classical domain of their Sages; nor have they reached the measured conception of the truth attained by the Greeks,—a conception limited to an apprehending of the unsatisfying inadequacy of a stoical philosophy and a soulless art.

Pending this higher law's fulfilment, we

are forbidden to stand still,—nay, we are not of the Stoics; and it seems a law of our nature, as it is the outcome of our Faith, that we desire the participation of others in our heritage. Such is the force of our human sympathy; but the impulse restrains the use of dogma, and implies, rather, a spirit of fellowship. And these reflections suggest that we shall do well not to oppose dogma to dogma in discussions with a people who are so firmly bound by dogma and a fixed system of Rites that to do so is to arouse controversy and exasperation, instead of conciliating opinion. Yet, when they extol the philosophical teachings of their Sages, as the limit at once of human conception and desire, we may impress upon them the healthful principle of human endeavor animated by human sympathy; that the culture of the heart, as of the mind, is the duty of a life,—that all Nature avouches the doom of inanition. The governing body and the literati generally are jealous of and naturally resent public teaching that offensively contradicts the venerated maxims of the Sages, as demonstrative of designs of a semi-political character.

There remains, finally, the effort to raise the peoples, each in their own section and by the use and improvement of their respective vernacular dialects, as the peoples of the various European Nations were raised by their discerning scholars and patriots, until they were so invigorated as to be able to cast off the thraldom linked with the Latin tongue.

The condition of the masses of the Chinese people in relation to the language of the governing body, and especially as regards the tenacious connection of that language with the ancient conjoint system of education and Government, is, as I have already implied, analogous to that of those European peoples at that period.

The Religions bonds holding those European peoples were, however, much stronger than any now holding the Chinese to any particular Faith or observances, with the exception of those of ancestral worship; and these are not matter of governmental concern or ecclesiastical cognizance, being voluntary, although imperative as a part of the social polity, in each individual or family.

But this system of ancestral worship is the real stronghold of the Chinaman's Faith. It seems to absorb what of warmth there is in his heart, beyond the mingled feeling of pride and affection that he evinces toward his son and successor in those duties.

Strip it of its idolatrous elements and it is commendable. Once that is done his cold, selfish, nature will no longer be barren of human sympathy, but will have become receptive of the Faith that is of and from the heart.

Already the light of Science is casting its beneficent rays into the labyrinthine darkness of the old routine, and the inert mass has felt some electrical shocks. Medical science has long been freely given; and along with it the teaching of Christian Missionaries. The measure of these largesses must impress the minds of the people.

Nor are we in doubt of this, for already two years ago the gentry of Canton practically acknowledged, in the most emphatic manner, the service that Foreigners had for nearly half a century freely accorded their afflicted countrymen, by following the example of establishing an Hospital of their own and also by employing members of the Literati to statedly read the Sacred Edict and promulgate the doctrines of the Sages.

Whether regarded as the outcome of a latent spirit of benevolence, tardily aroused to activity by the spectacle of the beneficent work of the Foreigners, or as a manifestation of the ever-present jealousy of the gentry of Foreign influence, it is equally a recognition of the deepening impression created upon the public mind.

All honor, then, to the faithful toilers in long-sterile fields.

It cannot be long before the people of the whole of the accessible parts of the Empire will acknowledge themselves thus enriched from the Western Nations.

Thenceforward the way will be clear,—the goal assured.

G. NYE.

ONE PAGE FROM CHOO FOO-TSZE.

朱子曰太極圖只是一箇實理
一以貫之○太極一圖便是一
畫只是撒開了引教長一畫○
無極而太極上一圖則是太極
但挑出在上○無極而太極此
五字添減一字不得○無極而
無中自有此理無極而太極此
而字輕無次序故也○無極而
太極只是說無形而有理所謂
太極者只二氣五行之理非別
有物爲太極也○以理言之則
不可謂之有以物言之則不可
謂之無○無極而太極正謂無
此形狀而有此道理耳○無
而太極正恐人將太極做一箇
有形象底看故又說無極只是
是此理也○無極而太極只是
一句如沖漠無朕畢竟是上面

無形象然却實有此理圖上自分曉○間：無極
且得做無形無象說曰雖無形却有理又間無
極太極只是一物日本是一物被他恁地說却
似兩物○無極是有理而無形如性何嘗有形
太極是五行陰陽之理皆有不是空底物事若
是空時如釋氏說性相似○極是道理之極至
總天地萬物之理便是太極○間無極而太極
固是一物有積漸否曰無積漸曰上言無極下
言太極竊疑上言無窮無極下言至此方極曰
無極者無形太極者有理也周子恐人把作一
物看故云無極曰太極既無形氣象如何曰只
是理○太極只是極至更無去處了至高至妙
至精至神是沒去處濂溪恐人道太極有形故
曰無極而太極是無之中有箇極至之理○間
無極而太極因而字故生陸氏議論曰而字自
分明下云動而生陽靜而生陰說一生字便見
其自太極來今日而則只是一理○老子之言
有無以有無爲二周子之言有無以有無爲一
性理大全太極圖第八篇

The following is a feeble attempt at a translation, but all who read Chinese are earnestly requested to give their attention to the original and compare it with what is said on page 85 of the last Number of the *China Review.*   J. C.

Choo-tsze said :—

1. (The idea of) 'the Plan of the Great Extreme' is but one positive Law—an all-pervading Unity.

2. The one circle of the Great Extreme is just a line, that is to say, one line drawn out and prolonged (makes the circle).

3. Respecting 'the Infinite and Great Extreme' the uppermost circle is the Great Extreme, only displaced so as to appear on the top of the Plan.

4. Of the five words "The Infinite and Great Extreme" not one can be spared; nor can one word be added thereto.

5. Respecting "The Infinite and Great Extreme," it is not meant that besides the Great Extreme there is a separate Infinite; but that in the non-existent there is the self-existent Law. In the phrase "The Infinite and Great Extreme" the word 'and' has a light meaning, there being no sequence intended.

6. "The Infinite and Great Extreme" means the non-existence of form and the existence of Law. What is called 'Great Extreme' is simply the Law of the Light and Dark Air and the Five Elements. There is not a separate thing constituting 'the Great Extreme.'

7. Spoken of as Law it cannot be said to have a (substantial) existence, but spoken of as a thing (a matter of fact) it cannot be said to be non-existent.

8. 'The Infinite and Great Extreme' just means the entire absence (non-existence) of form and manifestation, and the existence only of the Ultimate Principle (Reason-Law) of them.

9. Respecting 'The Infinite and Great Extreme,' there was a fear (on the part of Chow-tsze) that people would misunderstand 'the Great Extreme' as having somewhat of form or similitude, therefore it was also

defined (by him) to be 'The Infinite' that is to say the Law only.

10. 'The Infinite and Great Extreme' is only one phrase, the elements of which run together without any distinction of 'me' (and 'not me'). And, in fine, it denotes the entire absence of all form and similitude on the upper side of the Plan, while at the same time the positive Law exists. This is apparent on the face of the Plan itself.

11. To the remark of an inquirer, that 'The Infinite' may then be defined to be the entire absence of form or similitude, Choo replied " Though form exists not, still Law exists." Again the inquirer remarked (evidently puzzled) "'The Infinite,' 'the Great Extreme'—they are then one thing !" Upon which Choo said, "As the words originally stand one thing is meant; but when an individual uses them in that fashion they certainly seem to mean two things. (The individual had omitted the 'and').

12. 'The Infinite' means the existence of Law, and the non-existence of form. For example Nature, what form has it ever had ? 'The Great Extreme' means the universally existing Law of the Five Elements and the Light and Darkness. It is not something void (mere nothingness). If it were absolute vacuity then it would resemble the Buddhist definition of Nature (Nihilism).

13. 'Extreme' means the ultimate perfection of Law. Generalize all the Laws of Heaven and Earth and all things, and that is 'the Great Extreme.'

14. One inquired saying, "'The Infinite and Great Extreme' is, we will take for granted, one thing, but is it subject to any increase or variability?" Choo replied, "None." Again it was remarked, "In the former (upper) clause it is said to be Infinite (Limitless) and in the latter (lower) to be the Great Extreme (Grand Limit). Now I venture to doubt whether the meaning is not, that, while it is said above to be Boundless and Infinite, it is limited (or subject to limitation) downwards (towards the material side)." Choo said in reply, "'The Infinite'

means having no form, and 'the Great Extreme' means having Law. Chow-tsze was afraid that people would take it (the Great Extreme) to mean a Thing* (having form), therefore he said it was 'the Infinite.'" It was further asked, "'The Great Extreme' being as you say, formless, what about the figures of the Air (as shown in the Plan)?" Choo replied, "It is only the Law (of the figures)."

15. 'The Great Extreme' is the ultimate result of analysis beyond which it is impossible to go; most high, most beautiful, most subtile, most spiritual, so that there is no going beyond it. Chow Lien-k'i was afraid that people would say that 'the Great Extreme' had form, therefore he said 'The Infinite and Great Extreme,' that is to say, in non-existence there exists an ultimate Law.

16. An inquirer said, " The word 'and' in the expression 'The Infinite and Great Extreme' was probably what gave rise to the Speculations of Luh" (a man of Buddhistic tendencies. See above). Choo replied, "The word 'and' becomes of itself perfectly clear, when, in the next sentence, the text goes on to speak of moving and *producing* Light, resting and *producing* darkness. The moment the word *producing* comes in it is apparent that what follows proceeds from the Great Extreme; but here it is merely said 'and,' thence the one Law is all that is intended (by the whole phrase 'the Infinite and Great Extreme').

17. When Lau-tsze spoke of existence and non-existence he regarded them as *two ;* when Chow-tsze spoke of existence and non-existence he regarded them as *one.*

Note.—It is quite true that Lau-tsze said,

---

* 一 物 we cannot translate here 'one thing,' because the emphasis is evidently not on the numeral as in the previous cases, but on 'thing.' There was no need nor danger of people taking 'the Great Extreme' for *two* things. In fact that kind of danger was created by Chow-tsze's addition of 'the Infinite.' And a real danger it is, for some people have thought since that there are two Great Extremes.

"Tau produced Unity." This proposition Chou rejects as meaning that the *non-ens* produced the *ens*, as if "the Infinite" *produced* "the Great Extreme," whereas he held with Chow-tsze that these two terms mean 'one thing.'—Observe the use of the word 物 *wuh* throughout the page, having all the indefiniteness of our word 'thing.' It cannot be translated "Matter" (See *China Review*, Vol. III. p. 346, Vol. IV. p. 94.)

THE EXPEDITION OF THE MONGOLS AGAINST JAVA IN 1293, A.D.

It is generally known that Kublai, the first Emperor of the Mongol dynasty, which reigned over China under the name of Yüan, sent a military expedition to Java, shortly after his accession to the throne. As far as I am aware, however, no details about this important enterprise have ever been published; beyond the bare fact little seems to be known about it, and even this knowledge is unsatisfactory, as there is uncertainty about the date, whilst some European writers call it only an attack by Chinese pirates, not emanating from the Government at all, and others seem inclined to look upon it as an idle story altogether.

I have been engaged lately in collecting the different notices about the Malay archipelago which are found in Chinese sources, and, in doing so, have come across a detailed account of this expedition in the History of the Yüan dynasty; the publication of my compilation has been delayed by different circumstances and may be so for some time to come, for which reason I now venture to come before the public with this extract first.

As the History of the Yüan dynasty does not give the details of this expedition in one succinct narrative, but treats of it in the accounts of Java and in the biographies of the three generals who led the Mongol army, we think it the best plan to translate these different pieces first and to see afterwards what information may be derived from them,

by comparing them with each other as well as with other sources treating of the same subject.

ACCOUNT OF JAVA, HISTORY OF THE YUAN
DYNASTY, BOOK 210.

Java 爪哇 is situated beyond the sea and further away than Champa; when one embarks at Ch'üan-chou 泉州 and goes southward, he first comes to Champa and afterwards to this country.

The customs and products of this land are not much known, but as a rule the barbarian countries over the sea produce many rare and valuable things, which fetch a high price in China. The inhabitants are ugly and uncouth, their nature and speech are not understood by the Chinese.

When the emperor Shih-tsu (Kublai) pacified the barbarians of the four quarters of the world and sent officers to the different countries over the sea, Java was the only place he had to send an army to.

In the second month of the year 1292, 至元二十九年 the Emperor issued an order to the Governor of Fukien, directing him to send Shih-pi, Ike Mese and Kau Hsing in command of an army to subdue Java; to collect soldiers from Fukien, Kiangsi and Hukuang to the number of 20,000; to appoint a Commander of the Right Wing and one of the Left, as well as four Commanders of Ten Thousand; to send out a thousand ships and to equip them with pro visions for a year and with forty thousand bars of silver. The Emperor further gave ten tiger badges, forty golden badges and a hundred silver badges, together with a hundred pieces of silk embroidered with gold, all for the purpose of rewarding merit.

When Ike Mese and his associates had their last audience, the Emperor said to them: "When you arrive at Java you must clearly proclaim to the army and the people of that country, that the Imperial Government has formerly had intercourse with Java by envoys from both sides and has been in good harmony with it, but that they have lately cut the face of the imperial envoy Meng Ch'i 孟琪* and that you have come to punish them for that."

In the 9th month some troops were collected at Ch'ing-yüan (Ningpo); Shih-pi and Ike Mese went with the soldiers overland to Ch'üan-chou, whilst Kau Hsing brought the baggage with the ships. In the course of the 11th month the troops from the three provinces of Fukien, Kiangsi and Hukuang were all assembled at Ch'üan-chou, and in the next month the expedition put to sea. In the first month of the year 1293 they arrived at the island Kou-lan 枸欄山 (Billiton) and there deliberated on their plan of campaign.

In the second month Ike Mese and one of his subordinate commanders, taking with them their secretaries and accompanied by three officers of the Office of Pacification 宣慰司 (also written 宣撫司), who were charged to treat with Java and the other countries, and by a commander of ten thousand who led five hundred men and ten ships, went first in order to bring the commands of the Emperor to this country. The body of the army followed to Karimon 吉利門 (Karimon Java) and from here to a place on Java called Tu-ping-tsuh

*We may observe here that in the Chinese text of these accounts a number of subordinate officers are mentioned, all with their full names; as these names are of no use for our purpose and may fatigue the reader, we will omit them as much as possible.

杜並足 (Tuban), where Shih-pi and Kau Hsing met Ike Mese again and determined, together with the other leaders, that half the army should be sent ashore and the other half proceed at the same time in the ships. Shih-pi went by sea to the mouth of the river Sugalu 戎牙路 (Sedayu), and from there to the small river Pa-tsieh 八節門 (river of Surabaya). On the other hand Kau Hsing and Ike Mese led the rest of the troops, being cavalry and infantry, and marched from Tu-ping-tsuh overland, one of the Commanders of the Ten Thousand leading the vanguard. Three superior officers were sent in fast boats from the river Sugalu, with the order to go first to the floating bridge of Modjopait 麻喏巴歇 and then to rejoin the army on its way to the small river Pa-tsieh.

The Officers of the Office of Pacification soon reported that the son-in-law of the prince of Java, called Tuhan Pidjaya 土罕必闍耶, wished to make his country submit, but as he could not leave his army, orders were given to three officers to go and bring his prime minister Sih-la-nan-ta-ch'a-ya 昔刺難答吒耶 and fourteen others, who wanted to come and receive the army of the emperor.

On the 1st day of the 3rd month, the troops were assembled at the small river Pa-tsieh. This river has at its upper course the palace of the king of Tumapan 杜馬班 (Tumapel) and discharges itself into the sea called Pou-pên 莆奔, it is the entrance to Java and a place for which they were determined to fight. Accordingly the first minister of the Javanese, Hi-ning-kuan 希寗官 remained in a boat to see how the chances of the fight went; he was summoned repeatedly but would not surrender.

The commanders of the imperial army made a camp in the form of a crescent on the bank of the river and left the ferry in charge of a Commander of Ten Thousand; the fleet in the river and the cavalry and infantry on shore then advanced together, and Hi-ning-kuan, seeing this, left his boat and fled overnight, whereupon more than a hundred large ships, with devil's-heads on the stem, were captured.

Orders were now given to a strong force to guard the mouth of the river Pa-tsieh, and the body of the army then advanced.

Messengers came from Tuhan Pidjaya, telling that the king of Kalang 葛郎 had pursued him as far as Modjopait and asking for troops to protect him. Ike Mese and one of his lieutenants hastened to him in order to keep up his courage and another officer followed with a body of troops to Chang-ku 章 孤* for the purpose of assisting them. Kau-hsing advanced to Modjopait, but heard that it was not known whether the soldiers of Kalang were far or near, so he went back to the river Pa-tsieh; at last he got information from Ike Mese that the enemy would arrive that night and was ordered to go again to Modjopait.

On the 7th day the soldiers of Kalang arrived from three sides to attack Tuhan Pidjaya, and on the 8th day, early in the morning, Ike Mese led part of the troops to engage the enemy in the southwest, but he did not meet them. Kau Hsing fought with the enemy on the southeast and killed several hundreds of them, whilst the remainder fled to the mountains. Towards the middle of the day the enemy arrived also from the southwest; Kau Hsing met them again, and towards evening they were defeated.

On the 15th the army was divided into three bodies, in order to attack Ka-lang; it was agreed that on the 19th they would meet at Daha 苔 哈 and commence the battle on hearing the sound of the p'au.† A part of the troops ascended the river; Ike Mese proceeded by the eastern road and Kau

* Probably Changkir, on the Brantas or Surabaya river, near the top of the delta, afterwards an important place for Chinese commerce.

† 礟, this character has been used by the Chinese first to denote catapults and afterwards guns. I am not prepared to take it in the second sense, as I am not aware the Mongols or Chinese had firearms at the time. It probably was a kind of rocket, giving a sound sufficiently strong to be audible to three bodies of troops.

Hsing took the western, whilst Tuhan Pidjaya with his army brought up the rear. On the 19th they arrived at Daha, where the prince of Kalang defended himself with more than a hundred thousand soldiers. The battle lasted from six in the morning till two in the afternoon, and three times the attack was renewed, when the enemy was defeated and fled; several thousands thronged into the river and perished there, whilst more than 5,000 were slain. The king retired into the inner city, which was immediately surrounded by our army and the king summoned to surrender; in the evening the king, whose name was Hadji Katang 哈只葛當, came out of the fortress and offered his submission; on this the orders of the Emperor were delivered to him and he was told to go back.

On the 2nd day of the 4th month Tuhan Pidjaya was sent back to his dominions in order to make preparations for sending tribute; two officers and 200 soldiers went with him as an escort. On the 19th Tuhan Pidjaya secretly left our soldiers and attacked them, by which the whole party came to grief.

On the 24th the army went back, taking with it the wife, the children and officers of Hadji Katang, altogether more than a hundred persons; they brought also a map of the country, a register of the population and a letter in golden characters presented by the king.

For further particulars see the biography of Shih-pi.

ACCOUNT OF SHIH-PI, HISTORY OF THE YUAN DYNASTY, BOOK 162.

Shih-pi, whose literary name was Chün-tso and who was also called Tarhun 史 弼 字 君 佐 亦 名 塔 爾 渾, was a man from Po-yeh, district Li-chou, department Pau-ting, province Chih-li.

(The historian describes his military career and, arriving at that part of it which may interest us, goes on as follows:)

When the emperor Shih-tsu (Kublai)

wanted to subdue Java, he said to Shih-pi: "Among my officers there are few who have my full confidence, therefore I want to entrust this affair of Java to you." The other replied: "If the Emperor deigns to command His servant, how could he venture to be afraid for his person."

In the year 1292 he was made commander of the expedition to Java, whilst Ike Mese and Kau Hsing were appointed to assist him. The Emperor gave him a hundred and fifty stamped badges and two hundred pieces of silk in order to reward those who made themselves meritorious. In the 12th month he joined the other troops with 5,000 men and departed from Ch'üan-chou; the wind was strong and the sea very rough, so that the ships rolled heavily and the soldiers could not eat for many days. They passed the Sea of the Seven Islands 七洲洋 (the Paracels Islands) and the Long Reefs 萬里石塘 (Macclesfield Bank), they passed the land of the Giau-chi (Annam) and Champa, and in the first month of the next year they came to the Eastern Tung Islands 東董山 (Natuna?), the Western Tung Islands 西董山 (Anamba?) entered the Indian Sea 混沌大洋 and consecutively arrived at the Olive Islands 橄欖嶼 (Tambilan?), Karimata 假里馬荅 and Kou-lan 勾闌 (Billiton?), where they stopped and cut timber to make small boats for entering the rivers.

At that time Java carried on an old feud with the neighbouring country Kalang, and the king of Java, Hadji Ka-ta-nu-ka-la 哈只葛達那加剌, had already been killed by the prince of Kalang, called Hadji Katang. The son-in-law of the former, Tuhan Pidjaya, had attacked Hadji Katang, but could not overcome him; he had therefore retired to Modjopait, and when he heard that Shih-pi with his army had arrived, he sent envoys with an account of his rivers and seaports and a map of the country Kalang, offering his submission and asking for assistance.

Shih-pi then advanced with all his forces, attacked the army of Kalang and routed it completely, on which Hadji Katang fled back to his dominions.

Kau Hsing now said: "Though Java has submitted, still if it repents its decision and unites with Kalang, our army might be in a very difficult position and we do not know what might happen." Shih-pi therefore divided his army into three parts, himself, Kau Hsing and Ike Mese, each leading a division, and marched to attack Kalang. When they arrived at the fortified town Daha, more than a hundred thousand soldiers of Kalang came forward to withstand them. They fought from morning till noon, when the army of Kalang was routed and retired into the town to save itself. The Chinese army surrounded the town and soon Hadji Katang came forward to offer his submission; his wife, his children and officers were taken by the victors, who then went back.

Tuhan Pidjaya asked permission to return to his country in order to prepare a new letter of submission to the Emperor and to take the precious articles in his possession for sending them to court; Shih-pi and Ike Mese consented to this and sent two officers with 200 men to go with him. Tuhan Pidjaya killed the two officers on the way and revolted again, after which he availed himself of the circumstance that the army was returning to attack it from both sides. Shih-pi was behind and was cut off from the rest of the army, he was obliged to fight his way for 300 'li before he arrived at the ships; at last he embarked again and reached Ch'üan-chou after a voyage of 68 days.

Of his soldiers more than 3,000 men had died. The Emperor's officers made a list of the valuables, incenses, perfumeries, textures, etc., which he had brought and found them worth more than 500,000 taels of silver. He brought also to the Emperor a letter in golden characters from the country Muli (or Buli) 沒理, with golden and silver articles, rhinoceros-horns, ivory and other things.

(For more particulars see the articles on Kau Hsing and on Java.)

On account of his having lost so many men, the Emperor ordered Shih-pi to receive seventeen lashes, and confiscated a third of his property. In the year 1295 he was raised again to office, and a memorial was presented to the Emperor, pointing out that Shih-pi and his associates had gone over the sea to a distance of 25,000 *li*, had led the army to countries which had never been reached in the last reigns, had captivated a king and awed into submission the neighbouring small countries, and that, for these reasons, mercy should be shown to him.

The Emperor then restored his goods, which had been confiscated and raised him gradually to the highest ranks, until he died at the age of 86 years.

ACCOUNT OF KAU HSING, HISTORY OF THE
YUÁN DYNASTY, BOOK 162.

Kau Hsing, styled Kung-chi, was a man from Ts'ai-chou 高興字功起蔡州人.*

(The account gives a pretty long description chiefly of his military career, and then proceeds:)

When Java had marked the face of the Imperial envoy Mèng Ch'i, the Emperor appointed Kau Hsing, together with Shih-pi and Ike Mese, to take command of an army and go to subdue this country. He also got a girdle adorned with precious stones, embroidered garments, armour, a helmet, a bow and arrows and a thousand *mou* of good land near a large town.

In the beginning of the year 1293 they reached Java; Ike Mese took command of the fleet and Kau Hsing led the infantry, and at the small river Pa-tsieh they united again. As the son-in-law of the late King of Java, Tuhan Pidjaya, had offered his submission, they marched to attack, the country of Kalang, and subdued its king

* Ts'ai-chou is an old name for the present district 新蔡, department 汝寧, in the province of Honan.

Hadji Katang. (For further particulars see the article on Shih-pi.)

They also awed into submission different smaller states, and as Hadji Katang's son, Sih-lah-pat-tih-sih-lah-tan-puh-hah 昔剌八的昔剌丹不合 had fled to the mountains, Kau Hsing went into the interior with a thousand men and brought him back a prisoner.

When he returned to the fortified town Daha, Shih-pi and Ike Mese had already allowed Tuhan Pidjaya to go back to his country with an escort from the Imperial army, in order to make preparations for sending tribute. Kau Hsing disapproved of this very much, and indeed Tuhan Pidjaya killed the men sent with him, and revolted again; he collected a large quantity of soldiers to attack the Imperial army, but Kau Hsing and the others fought bravely with him, and threw him back. After this they killed Hadji Katang and his son and returned to China.

By an imperial decree Shih-pi and Ike Mese, who had allowed the prince of Java to go away, were punished, but as Kau Hsing had taken no part in this decision and moreover had greatly distinguished himself, the Emperor rewarded him with 50 taels of gold.

ACCOUNT OF IKE MESE,* HISTORY OF THE
YUÁN DYNASTY, BOOK 131.

Ike Mese 伊克穆蘇 also written 亦黑迷失 was a man from the land of the Uigurs.

In the year 1265, he entered the office of the Night Guard.

In the year 1272, he was sent by the Emperor across the sea as an envoy to the kingdom Pa-lo-p'ei (?) 八羅孛; he came back in 1274, bringing with him people of this country, who carried precious articles,

* This account is translated *in extenso*, because it shows in what way and for what purposes intercourse with foreign countries was carried on at the time.

and a letter of tribute. The Emperor praised him and gave him a golden tiger badge.

In the year 1275, he went again to the same country and brought back a functionary who offered a famous medicine to the Emperor; on this occasion he got again most valuable presents.

In 1277 he became a vice-president of the board of war.

In 1281 he was made resident of King-hu 荆湖 and Champa 占城.

In 1284 he was recalled and sent again across the sea as an envoy to Singhala 僧迦剌 (Ceylon), in order to inspect the alms'-bowl (pàtra) and other relics of Buddha; the Emperor gave him a precious girdle, dresses and horse trappings.

In 1285 he came back from his voyage, and was appointed Resident at the Court of the King of Chin-nan 鎮南.* Again a precious girdle was bestowed on him. Whilst in this office he made war against Champa, together with two other generals; they were defeated and one of the Generals killed. Ike Mese then told the king of Chin-nan to collect soldiers at the monastery of the High-waved Lake, in order to be able to move again. His orders were obeyed by the king, and so he succeeded in saving his army and came back.

In 1287 he was sent to the kingdom of Mapar (?) 馬八爾, to get the alms'-bowl and other relics of Buddha. On his voyage he had adverse winds, and it took him a year to arrive there. He succeeded in obtaining clever physicians and excellent medicines, and came back with people of the country bringing tribute. From his own money he had bought boards of red sandal-wood in order to make a pavilion for the Emperor; these he presented also.

Once, as he waited on the Emperor in his bathroom, the Emperor asked him how many times he had crossed the ocean. He answered, four times. The Emperor took pity on all his hardships, and gave him again a

girdle ornamented with jade, and the title of Minister of Accumulated Virtue.

Next he was appointed Governor residing at Ch'uan-chou 泉州, and in 1292 he was called to Court, on which occasion he presented to the Emperor all the precious articles in his possession. At that time an expedition against Java was contemplated, and an army for the purpose formed in Fukien. Ike Mese, together with Shih-pi and Kau Hsing, got the command of it; the formation of the army was entrusted to Shih-pi, whilst Ike Mese had to provide for the transport over sea.

The Emperor gave them the following instructions: "When you have arrived in Java, you must send a messenger to inform me of it. If you occupy that country, the other smaller states will submit from themselves, you have only to send envoys to receive their allegiance. When those countries are brought to obedience it will all be your work."

When the army arrived at Champa* they first sent envoys to call into submission Lambri, Sumatra, Pu-lu-pu-tu, Palala† and other small countries, and in the beginning of 1293 they defeated the country of Katang and subdued its king Hadji Katang. Another envoy was sent to the different Malay 木來由 states, who all sent their sons or younger brothers as a token of their allegiance.

The son-in-law of the prince of Java, Tuhan Pidjaya, submitted at first, but when he returned to his country he revolted again (for which see the account of Shih-pi).

The generals thought of carrying on the war, but Ike Mese wished to do as the

---

* According to the other accounts the army did not go to Champa, but only passed it; the meaning of this passage will be that, when the expedition was off Champa, a ship was detached from the fleet with the envoy for Sumatra, whose way lay along the coast, whilst the body of the army went on straight to Java.

† 南巫里 on the West coast of Sumatra, 速木都剌 the present Acheen. 不魯 不都 and 八剌剌 are not identified.

---

* At that time a small semi-independent state in the present province Yün-nan.

Emperor had ordered them, and first send a messenger to court. The two others could not agree to this, therefore the troops were withdrawn and they returned with their prisoners and with the envoys of the different smaller states which had submitted.

The Emperor reprimanded Ike Mese as well as Shih-pi, because they had allowed Tuhan Pidjaya to escape, and confiscated one third of his property, but this was soon restored to him.

Not long afterwards he retired from office on account of his age, and the Emperor, as a reward for his distant and difficult missions, gave him the title of Prince of Wu. He did not enjoy it long, but died soon afterwards.

———

Before pointing out what information may be derived from the four preceding accounts, we think it advisable to state in a few words what we know about that epoch from other sources.

In Raffles' *History of Java*, Vol. II., p. 110, we find the following account, drawn from a Balinese manuscript, which had been obtained a short time before Raffles wrote.

"Sri Laksi Kirana, King of Tumapel, left two sons, the elder named Sang Sri Siwa-buda and the younger Raden Wijaya. Sri Siwabuda was killed by Sri Jaya Katong, King of Kediri, who conquered the country and compelled Wijaya to fly. The latter afterwards collected a number of adherents around him, founded the new town of Moja-pahit, and soon was so strong that he thought of attacking Kediri. Some time before this the King of Tatar had been at Kediri, and Jaya Katong had promised him his daughter in marriage; as he delayed fulfilling this promise, the King of Tatar became angry, and hearing that Wijaya was going to attack Kediri, he proposed to join him. Wijaya accepted the proposal, the King of Tatar came with his army, and Jaya Katong was killed by him in battle with his own hand. After this the Tatar king went back to his country, and Wijaya reigned at Moja-

pahit, extending his sway over the whole island."

The same tradition, and probably from the same source, is mentioned by Friederich in his *Vooroopig verslag van het eiland Bali.*

The traditions current in Java are rather at variance with these details. Tumapel is not mentioned, and the ruling country in the eastern part of the island is called Djengolo. The names of the different persons disagree also, and the only point of similarity is that Djengolo is said to have been destroyed by the chief of the Kalangs, who is however called Boko. *Vide* Hageman, *Geschiedenis crz-van Java*, Deel I., p. 14.

In utilising these various accounts it must be remembered that the Chinese version is a sober narrative of facts, disfigured, it is true, by many errors and inaccuracies, but free from all fiction. The Balinese account has been handed down through many generations, gradually losing in accuracy and becoming mixed with much of the fantastic and marvelous, whilst Javanese tradition has been violently interrupted by the introduction of the Islam and, having been raked up from its embers at a later period, hardly seems to deserve any credit at all.

Returning now to our translations, we find that the Mongol prince Kublai, having rendered himself master of China, at once adopted the Chinese tradition of universal dominion, and accordingly sent envoys all over the world, as far as he was aware of its existence, informing the various princes that a new family had ascended the throne of the world and asking them to renew their allegiance.

The King of Tumapel in the eastern part of the island of Java, whose country was called by the Chinese Java *par excellence*, because it was in this part of the island they chiefly traded,* seems not to

* The name of Tumapel however is mentioned by the Chinese also. In the account of Java, translated above, it is said that the palace of the King of Tumapan (Tumapel) was situated on the upper course of the Surabaya river. We should say this was not quite correct, as the Mongol

have recognised these claims; he cut or tattooed the face of the imperial envoy and sent him away in this ignominious state. It is not stated in what year this happened, but we have seen already that Kublai, though dating his reign back to 1260, did not become undisputed master of China before 1280, and as, moreover, he was not a man to brook an insult long, we may assume that this envoy's visit to Java occurred not many years before 1292, when this expedition was sent to revenge the outrage.

The fleet sailed from Ch'üan-chou in Fukien, and did not follow the accustomed course along the coasts of Malacca and Sumatra, but kept further off, boldly taking the shortest road to its destination. For this reason the islands they passed on the middle of their course are not mentioned anywhere else, and we have not been able to identify them with absolute certainty, but the fact of their coming near Karimata sufficiently shows what must have been their route. They next came to an island which they call Kou-lan or Kô-lan, where they went ashore to repair their vessels and also made some smaller craft for entering the rivers; we cannot again identify this name, but as the island was situated between Karimata and Karimon Java, we may safely say that it was Billiton.

During this delay the political agents who accompanied the army went first to Java, to see what could be done by negociations, and the army soon followed, going first to the island Karimon Java and next to a place on Java's coast, which is called Tu-ping-tsuh.

The latter name looks thoroughly un-Javanese, and as it occurs only once in the narrative, it may be that the Chinese characters, used for its transcription, have become corrupted. Later Chinese geograph-

army ascended this river as far as Daha in Kediri, but do not seem to have found it on their way. Instead of on we have probably to read *near*, and this royal residence may have been situated on the site of the present village of Tumapel, on the upper course of the Tangi river.

ers and Chinese tradition in Java, all agree in identifying it with Tuban in Rembang, on the north coast of Java.

At this place Tuban sent half of |the army ashore, with orders to march towards the mouth of the river Pa-tsieh, whilst the other half proceeded in the fleet to the same destination, passing on its way the river Segalu (Su-ga-lu) which must be the same as is called Sedayu now. Pa-tsieh is the river of Surabaya, at present called Brantas or Kali Mas, which is proved beyond any doubt by the fact of Changku or Changko (afterwards an important place for Chinese trade and called Changkir by the natives) being situated on it, whilst it led also to the neighbourhood of Modjopait and to Daha in Kediri. The Chinese text gives this river as Pa-tsieh-kan 八節澗, *i. e.* the small river Pa-tsieh, and this name we find also in the village Patjekan of the present day, situated on its right bank, about nine miles from the sea. It is probable that formerly this village gave its name to the Surabaya branch of the Brantas.

The two divisions of the Mongol-Chinese army rejoined at the mouth of this river on the 1st day of the 3rd month (between half April and half May), but in the meantime information had been received that the king of Tumapel in Java, whom the expedition had come to punish, had been killed by his neighbour Adji Katang (or Katong),[*] king of the Kalang (or Kalong) people, who reigned at Daha in the present Kediri. The

[*] The Chinese text has Adji (or Hadji) Katang (or Katong), whilst the Balinese account gives Sri Java Katong. Of course this Adji does not mean here a Mahomedan who has made the pilgrimage to Mecca, but it was a title very common amongst the Hindus in Java.

His opponent, Raden Widjaya in the Balinese account, is called Tuban Widjaya by the Chinese. This Tuban is decidedly an Arab appellation and cannot have been used by a Javanese prince of that time. We explain this anachronism by assuming that the expedition was accompanied by Arabs from Canton, who served as interpreters and bestowed this title on Raden Widjaya. It is also possible that Arab merchants were already established on the coast of the island, and that they too designated him by this name.

territory of Tumapel had been conquered by
Adji Katang, only the son-in-law of the late
king, Raden Widjaya, was still in arms
against the invader and defended himself at
Modjopait,* which place he had founded as
a basis for his resistance.

These circumstances explain why the
Mongol troops did not meet with any resistance on their march from Tuban to the
mouth of the Surabaya river; the country
through which they passed had just suffered
all the horrors of a native war, and both
parties had collected all their available
forces in the south, where the last struggle
was going on.
Raden Widjaya offered his submission to
the Mongol generals, and sent some trusty
followers, who gave the necessary information about the roads, rivers and resources of
the country. Adji Katang, who was master
of the delta of Surabaya, assumed a hostile
attitude towards the foreign invaders, and
the Mongols found there an army which
tried to opposed them. The Mongol generals
therefore gladly accepted the assistance of
Raden Widjaya, and soon fought their first
battle at the mouth of the river Patsich,
where the Kalang troops were easily routed.
These troops, which seem to have been
under command, not of Adji Katang himself, but of one of his ministers, retired into
the interior and seem to have joined the
army of Adji Katang before Modjopait.

* Modjopait must therefore have been founded between the visit of the Mongol envoy Meng
Ch'i, say 1280 (but probably later) and the arrival of the expedition in 1293. This place has
been the last stronghold of Hinduism in Java,
and its ruins are still found in the district of
Modjokerto, belonging to the residency of Surabaya.

Raden Widjaya at least sent word that he
was sorely pressed by his foe and asked for
assistance. The Mongol army accordingly
marched in that direction, and a strong body
of troops was sent ahead to keep up the
spirits of their ally. On the 8th day of the
3d month a battle took place under the walls
of Modjopait; the Kalang army was defeated
and thrown back into the mountains south
of that place.

Not satisfied with this success the victors
now marched on Daha, the capital of Adji
Katang, which was attacked and captured
on the 19th day of the same month; the
king was made a prisoner and seems to have
been ultimately killed.

All resistance being now at an end, it
became Raden Widjaya's turn to pay for
the services, which the Mongol army had
rendered him; as however his opponent was
dead and the force of his country broken, he
did not require those services any more and
sought to avoid his obligations. He therefore pretended that he had to go back to his
capital in order to prepare adequate presents
for the emperor, and was allowed to depart
for this purpose, escorted by a few Chinese
troops. On his way he threw off the mask,
the Chinese escort was treacherously mas-
sacred, and he at once began hostilities
against his former allies. By this time the
Mongol generals had found out how difficult
it was to carry on war in these parts; they
did not think it advisable to begin a new
struggle, and, taking with them the more
important prisoners from Daha and whatever treasure they could collect, they returned to their ships and left the island
after a stay of about four months.

W. P. GROENEVELDT.

THE WRY-NECKED TREE.

At the foot of Prospect Hill stands an old
    distorted tree ;
'Neath its shade have often walked the
    Mings in all their pride.
It saw the first and last of that mighty
    dynasty,
For 'twas planted by *Yung-lo*, and on it
    Ch'ung-chên died.

Though leafless and distorted now, it was
    not always so ;
Its foliage was luxuriant, its trunk was tall
    and straight ;
Now, 'tis called the Wry-necked Tree, for
    two hundred years ago
The old tree bent its haughty head beneath
    a monarch's weight.

Two hundred years ago
What an awful stir
There must have been
'Neath the Wry-necked Fir,
When at dawn was seen
The corse of *Ch'ung-chên*
In the bright morning sun,
As it swayed on a branch to and fro.
Yes, it is he !
The corse that swings
On the Wry-necked Tree
Is the last of the Mings.
His race, alas ! is run ;
No more will he
Sway with his single Will,
Or govern the destiny,
Of " all beneath the sun."
At the foot of Prospect Hill,
The last of a dynasty,

A king—the " Solitary One "—
Hangs on the Wry-necked Tree.

It must have been
A strange sight
To have seen
At morning light
The corse of a king
From the old tree swing.

Every one near
Shuddered with awe,
And paled with fear
At the sight they saw ;
The white ghastly face
Of the last of his race
Seemed to look down,
From the old tree's bough,
On the group with a frown
And a lowering brow.
Lower it gently—the corse that swings
On the Wry-necked Tree is the last of the
    Mings.

Who knows what was said
At the last parting scene
Of *Ch'ung Chên* and his queen,*
Ere barefoot he fled
In the dead of the night,
Nor stayed in his flight
Till he reached the old tree
On which he now swings ?
Fulfilling his destiny ;
Last of the Mings.

* Tradition says that the empress committed
suicide, and the princess her daughter was slain
by the Emperor to prevent her falling into the
hands of the rebels.

Untold in History 's
His parting with her;
Shrouded in mystery 's
His death on the fir.
The last hours of Ch'ung Chên
Are known only to One.

When lowered to the ground,
In his breast
A paper was found,
Thus addressed:
"To Li-tzu-ch'êng,
When I am found dead,
On the fir tree hung,
Let this paper be read.
These our last wishes are written by Us."
The paper was opened; the writing ran thus:
Imperial brother, Li-tzu-ch'êng, I most devoutly pray
That if there *must* be slaughter, you'll *all* my courtiers slay;
But, oh! my loyal subjects, my black-haired people spare,
On no account slay them—grant this my earnest prayer.'

What shall be done
With the tree
Which hung Ch'ung Chên?
Which dared
Bear such imperial fruit?
Shall it be spared,
Or grubbed up by the root,
And die with the dynasty?
The tree that has gained
Such unholy renown
Shall not be cut down;
Let the culprit be chained.*
It thus shall remain
Till the end of time,
Bound with a chain
For its awful crime.
When the old fir tree
Shall be freed from its thrall,
The Ch'ing dynasty
Will totter and fall.†
May such a catastrophe never occur
As removing the chain from the Wry-necked Fir.

G. C. STENT.

* The actual words of the paper as given in the song are:—

拜上拜上多拜上
拜上皇兄李自成
要殺殺我文合武
千萬別殺好黎民

The rebel Li-tzu-chêng lived in the palace eighteen days. He had sufficient respect for the deceased emperor to place him in his coffin and sacrifice to him.

* Shun-chih, the first emperor of the Ch'ing dynasty, ordered the tree to be chained. He also granted permission to inter the body of the emperor in the family tomb.

† It is believed that should the tree be ever unchained, great calamity would befal the reigning dynasty. To this day the tree remains chained, but it has almost fallen to the ground.

PHALLIC WORSHIP.

[It is scarcely necessary to warn the reader that in bringing this charge of immoral teaching against Confucianism Canon MacClatchie stands entirely alone, unsupported either by native authority or foreign Sinologues, relying on the construction which he himself puts on the metaphysical speculations of the Yih-king, and most especially one passage, where a certain phrase is used, which in ancient Chinese had not the impure meaning which modern idioms have connected with it. We give insertion to this article with a view to induce some one to thoroughly exhibit the fallacy of the Canon's arguments as contained in his "Confucian Cosmogony" and other papers.—Ed. *China Review*.]

In his Aryan Mythology Cox[*] introduces his investigation of this subject with the following remarks: "The recognition of beings powerful enough to injure, and perhaps placable enough to benefit the children of men, involved the necessity of a worship or cultus. They were all of them gods of life and death, of reproduction and decay, of the great mystery which forced itself upon the thoughts of men from infancy to old age. . . . The words in which Æschylos and Shelley speak of the marriage of the heaven and the earth, do but throw a veil of poetry over an idea which might easily become coarse and repulsive, while they point unmistakeably to the crude sensuousness which adored the principle of life under the signs of the organs of reproduction in the world of animals and vegetables. . . . It is clear that such a cultus as this would carry with it a constantly increasing danger, until the original character of the emblem should be as thoroughly disguised as the names of some of the Vedic deities when transferred to Hellenic soil."

From the statements of the Yih King, and

* Vol. II., p. 112.

of Confucius in his Commentary,[*] Khoeu-khwăn or Shang-te is evidently the phallic God of Heathendom represented unmistakeably by the usual symbols. Khëen or his Male portion is the membrum virile, and Khwăn or his Female portion is the pudendum muliebre; [†] and these two are enclosed in the circle, or ring, or phallos, the "Great Extreme" or globe of Air (氣) *from* and *by* which, as "Great Monad" (太一), all things are generated and governed. The passages in the Yih King which contain the words of Confucius, although committed to memory in schools where the pupils are sufficiently advanced to be able to study this classic, are never *explained* by the teachers, but are passed over lest they should suggest improper thoughts. This statement rests upon the authority of schoolmasters themselves, whose integrity on this point there appears no reason to question; and the

* E. gr. The 泰 Diagram. Also Bk. III. 上, Ch. vi., and 下 Ch. vi. See also *Confucian Cosmogony*, pp. 57, (par. 7, 8, 9,) 71, (37), 152.

† See Morrison & Williams (陰 and 陽).

authority assigned for this practice is the saying of Confucius that "There are three things which the Model Man guards against. In youth, when the physical powers are not yet settled, he guards against lust;" &c.[*] The law laid down by Confucius in the Le Ke[†] is that the children of opposite sexes in families should not be allowed to sit and eat together at table after the age of seven years.

The following description of the Altar of Heaven or the Male Phallos at Peking, is given in the "Digest of Laws" of the present Dynasty:—[‡]

皇 冬 三 圜 以 於 禮 凡
天 至 成 丘 象 南 兆 郊
上 日 歲 其 天 郊 陽 天
帝 祀 以 制 日 圓 位 之

"The symbol of the Male throne, where all the sacrifices are offered to Heaven, is in the southern suburb; it is round to resemble Heaven, and is called the round sacrificial Mound. It consists of three terraces; and every year, at the winter solstice, Imperial Heaven, the Supreme Emperor, is worshipped here."

The following is the description of the Altar of Earth or the Female Phallos, given in the same work:—

祇 日 水 以 二 方 於 禮 凡
祭 以 方 成 澤 北 兆 祭
皇 瘞 坎 四 其 郊 陰 地
地 至 蓍 周 制 日 位 之

"The symbol of the Female throne, where all the sacrifices are offered to Earth, is in the northern suburb, and is called the square sacrificial pool. It consists of two terraces surrounded on the four sides by a trench filled with water, and at the summer solstice the Goddess Empress Earth is here sacrificed to."

In these two altars, the "symbols" of the

male and female principles, and on which the phallic God Heaven with his wife Earth are sacrificed to, we have evidently the Linga and Yoni of the Hindus, the shape of the latter being generally regarded as square in China and oval in India. Both these emblems are frequently combined in China as they are amongst the Hindus; and this combination is seen in the pagoda and the single as well as triple and other mounds on graves, each of which stands upon a square base to represent Earth, while the pagoda or mound represents Heaven.

The round form of the female phallos is however seen in the Chinese "Great Extreme" or entire body of Air (氣) when in its mixed or chaotic state, in which it is female or yin, and is represented by a circle or ring,[*] the firstborn deity from which is Imperial Heaven or the male Shang-te, who then like Jupiter or Heaven is united in marriage to the Earth, his Mother;[†] and these two Deities then become the Great Father and Mother of all things; "Confucius said, 'If Heaven and Earth did not pair together (合) the myriad of things could not be generated[‡].'" When the Air divides from its chaotic state into the yin and yang, both of these principles are included in the ring or circle or globe[§].

The symbol or Linga of Imperial Heaven is also seen in the T'ae (泰) Mountain, worshipped by the Emperors of China from the highest antiquity and which is supposed to be animated by the divine soul (神, τὸ θεῖον) of Shang-te;[‖] for which reason it is designated "the Ancestor of all other mountains." Every year, in the second month, the ancient Emperors proceeded eastward on a tour of inspection and offered a burnt sacrifice to this T'ae Ancestor.[¶] This burnt sacrifice, we are told, was peculiar to Heaven

---

* Dr. Legge's Lun Yu, p. 176 and note.
† See V., p. 68.
‡ 欽定大清會典, Sec. 37.

* See Cox, Vol. II., p. 115. Confucian Cosmogony, Plate II., and p. 155.
† Confucian Cosmogony, p. 144.
‡ Le Ke, Sec. III., p. 40.
§ Confucian Cosmogony, p. 155.
‖ Lun Yu, p. 20, and note, (Legge).
¶ See Shoo King, Vol. I., sec. i., p. 12 and Com.

or Shang-te and is the 旅 sacrifice which is offered to him on the Altar of Heaven at Peking " in time of calamity." * The crime which the chief of the Ke family was about to commit, and which Confucius rebuked, did not consist in the *mere* worship of this Mountain, for all the Chinese throughout the Empire worship it, but in attempting to offer the 旅 sacrifice, which could only be offered by the Emperor, or the Prince of the State if deputed by him. The people of Shanghae burn incense to this Ancestral Mountain from the 23rd to the 28th of the third month.

Confucius tells us in the Le Ke that "the burnt sacrifices at the T'ac Altar are offered to Heaven ; and the buried funeral sacrifices at the T'ac Hollow are offered to Earth." The T'ac Altar, we learn from the Commentary, is "the round sacrificial Mound 丘 ;" and the T'ac Hollow is "the square sacrificial Hollow Space 丘." The 折 is the hollow place in the small square at the top of the Altar of Earth in which the sacrifices to the goddess are "buried." Confucius states that "when the myriad of things are *dead* they are called 折 ;" and hence the term "buried" applied to these sacrifices.† The term "T'ac" applied to the two Altars is significant ; for, on turning to that Diagram in the Yih King, we find that it refers to wealth and abundance, and represents the period when Imperial Shang-te and his wife Empress Earth unite together for the production of all things.

The character of the sacrifices offered at the Altar of Earth is worthy of notice. Khwăn as the *Yĭn* principle or Darkness is the agent of destruction at the end of each Kalpa, represented by the Pŏh Diagram, during which period Shang-te or the male principle is enveloped in the Darkness.|

The Hindus, writes Mr. Wilford, "represent Narayana, *moving* (as his name implies) *on the waters*, in the character of the *first male*, and the *principle* of all nature, which was wholly surrounded in the beginning by *Tamasa* or darkness : the *chaos* or primordial night of the Greek mythologists, and, perhaps, the *Thaumaz* or *Thamas* of the ancient *Egyptians*." * Hence, as the *Yĭn* is also Hades, the sacrifices at this female symbol at Peking, are regarded as funereal, and as being "buried" in the womb of the Earth, in which, as a ship or "Receptacle," all things are stored up while the chaotic flood prevails, and from which they are generated anew when the waters subside ; hence the title 廣生 or "the Capacious Generatrix" given to Khwăn or Earth. As this *Yĭn* is the Mother† of Imperial Heaven or the *Yang* as well as his wife, this Shang-te or Khĕen is the very Tammuz or Adonis wept for at the circular Altar of Baal-peor, "the Priapos of the Jews" at the period of "the winter solstice."‡ Of this fact we have an indubitable corroboration in the prohibition, by Confucius himself, of all lamentation *during the sacrifices to the Imperial Heaven ; e.gr.* " During the sacrifices to Heaven, mourning for the dead is strictly prohibited," § &c. Here then we have the *cultus* plainly separated from impure *ritual*. To worship the phallic God Shang-te with burnt sacrifices, on his symbol, is unquestionably phallic worship ; but such *cultus* by no means necessarily implies the use of impure orgies such as those practised by the Hindus. On this point Mr. Cox writes as follows ; "Even when the emblems still retain more or less manifestly their original character, the moral

---

* Williams' *Lex.*
† Sec. viii., pp. 26, 27. For the double meaning of 丘 see Morrison ; 丘子 is the *hollow* vault in which the coffin is placed ; erected *on* the ground ; see Williams.
‡ *Confucian Cosmogony*, Plate II., and p. 55, (par. 6).

* Moor's *Hindu Pantheon* (Simpson), p. 303.
† 性理大全 Sec. xi.
‡ Cox, Vol., II., p. 113. According to the Yih King he returns on the *seventh* day, and hence funeral rites are performed in periods of seven days : seven sevens or forty-nine days in all. Tammuz was supposed to return on the *third* day.
§ 郊之祭也喪者不敢哭 (lit. *dare not*, &c.) *Le Ke*, Sec. viii., p. 39.

effect on the people varies greatly, and the coarser developments of the cultus are confined to a comparatively small number. Professor Wilson says that it is unattended in Upper Egypt by any indecent or indelicate ceremonies."[*] The Chinese, who resemble the Egyptians in this absence of an impure ritual based on their phallic *cultus*, in fact regard the veneration paid to their phallic Deities, and the sacrifices offered to them at Peking, upon the quiescent and energising phallos as perfectly natural, and as being "a recompense paid to origin." Even amongst the Hindus, where an abominable ritual exists, Sir W. Jones remarks that "it seems never to have entered into the heads of the Hindu legislators and people that anything natural could be offensively obscene—a singularity which pervades all their writings, but is no proof of the depravity of their morals; hence the worship of the Linga by the followers of Siva, and of the Yoni by the followers of Vishnu."[†] "It may seem strange," writes Mr. Wilford in reference to the war between the two sects, "that a question of mere physiology should have occasioned, not only a vehement religious contest, but even a bloody war; yet the fact appears to be historically true, though the Hindu writers have dressed it up, as usual, in a veil of extravagant allegories and mysteries which we call obscene, but which they consider as awfully sacred."[‡]

In his Hindu Pantheon Moor gives a plate representing "a pious female propitiating Mahadeva in his generative character, indicated by the Linga inserted in its appropriate receptacle the Argha or Yoni, &c. The devout female may be imagined as invoking the deities typified by their symbols[§] &c. And, as in the case of the Chinese *yin* and *yang*, so also of this Linga and Yoni we learn from Muir's Sanscrit texts, that

"this whole world moveable and immoveable is pervaded by these two bodies."[*] Hence Milton alluding to this tenet of pagandom says:

"——and other suns, perhaps,
With their attendant moons thou wilt descry,
Communicating male and female light,
Which two great sexes animate the world."
Paradise Lost, Bk. viii. 148 &c.

The Chinese term *yang* corresponds to the term "Linga;" and the term *yin* to the term "Yoni," and also to the Latin term "Juno;" these three, in the material system, being not only the designations of the symbol of Goddess Earth, but also being regarded as the Earth herself. "If the Linga," writes Mr Cox, "is the sun god in his majesty, the Yoni is the Earth who yields her fruit under his fertilizing warmth, and it thus represents the sum of all potential existence."[†] The Stoical Juno as well as the Chinese *yin* is the Air from which the Earth is eventually formed, which was regarded by them as being soft and feminine.[‡] And, as all the Deities of the Chinese pantheon are the offspring of Imperial Heaven and his wife Empress Earth, they are all regarded as having sexes; *e. gr.* "The Celestial Gods are all of the masculine gender . . . . The Terrestrial Deities are all of the feminine gender."[§] Hence the ridicule thrown upon the pagan Deities by the Christian Arnobius tells with full force against the Imperial Shang-te, Empress Earth, and their whole Divine progeny; "Habent Dii sexus, et genitalium membrorum circumferunt feeditates? O pura, O sancta, atque ab omni turpitudinis labe disparata divinitas! Lubet videre Deas gravidas, Deas fœtas," &c.[‖]

The full force of the application of this satire to all the 神 of China, from Impe-

---

[*] Cox, Vol. II., p. 112 *note*.
[†] Cox, Vol. II., p. 112 *note*.
[‡] Moor's *Hind. Panth.*, p. 302.
[§] Page 47.

[*] Moor's *Hind. Panth.*, p. 300.
[†] Vol. ii., p. 118.
[‡] Cic. *De Naturâ Deorum*, p. 68. (Bohn's Class. Lib.) and Cud. Intell. Syst. Vol. ii., pp. 150, 224.

[§] 天神皆陽類也 ‥‥ 地祇皆陰類也·
[‖] See *Conf. Cosmog.*, p. 152.

rial Shang-te and his wife Empress Earth downwards, as well as to all the western Dii from the Kingly Jupiter and his Queen Earth downwards, must be fully apparent to all but those who have a favourite theory, handed down by tradition, to support; and who are not scrupulous as to the means to be adopted to gloss over or crush if possible the weight of evidence which they have no desire to investigate impartially. True wisdom in this case, would consist, not in endeavouring to explain away, or in omitting from publications the plain and unmistakeable statements of the Confucian classics, but in following the advice of Origen in his remarks upon the obscene picture of Jupiter (Heaven) and Juno (Earth) in Samos; that Father observes, "For the sake of which, and innumerable other such-like fables, we will never endure to call the God over all by the name of Jupiter (or *Shang-te*), but, exercising pure piety towards the maker of the world, will take care not to defile divine things with impure names." *

Another symbol of the phallic Deity of heathendom is the serpent or dragon;† and Imperial Heaven or Shang-te is also represented under this symbol ; *e. gr.* " Wăn the Duke of Tsin having dreamed that a yellow snake descended from heaven and came in contact with the earth, while it's mouth pointed to the hills of Foo, made enquiries of the historian Tun, who said, 'This is a proof of the presence of Shang-te; your Highness should sacrifice to him.' On this

account he constructed an altar at Foo, and using the three kinds of sacrificial animals, he offered the great sacrifice to the White Emperor." * Hence also the serpent was worshipped by the Chinese Viceroy resident at Tëen-tsin during the floods which occurred there in 1873.

In the Khëen Diagram of the Yih King,† we are told that the Dragon is " the subtile ether," and also that Khëen or Shang-te is the " most pure and subtile ether ;" the Dragon therefore is the same as Shang-te, both being the *yang* 氣. Hence we are told that; "The Dragon is the membrum virile." "The symbol of Khëen is the Dragon." "The Diagram of the pure Male is Khëen, and he is symbolized by the Dragon."§ And, as Khëen or Imperial Heaven with his wife Khwăn or Earth are the patrons of production and generation, they are always worshipped at marriages. Hence the term Dragon " is often used for *a man* in matters *relating to betrothals ;* and the phrase 乘龍 is used for "getting married." ‡ The story of Bel and the Dragon is founded on this superstition, which comes down from Babylon, and the reproduction of it in China proves Khëen or Shang-te to be the very Baal of the Chaldeans, the symbol of both these Deities being the serpent or Dragon, which represents the Male nature.

THOS. McCLATCHIE.

* Cud., Vol. ii., p. 254.
† Cox., Vol., ii., p. 116.

* Medhurst's *Shoo King*, p. 397.
† Ch. 32, 39.
‡ Yih King, Vol., ii. Sec. i., p. 4 (Imp. Ed.)
§ See Williams' *Lex.* Shang-te therefore is *unmistakeably* the God *Priapus.*

SHORT NOTICES OF NEW BOOKS*

AND LITERARY INTELLIGENCE.

Transactions of the Asiatic Society of Japan.
Vol. III., Part II. Yokohama, 1875.
Printed at the *Japan Mail* Office.

The volume before us displays an abundance of literary power which argues well for the future of the Asiatic Society of Japan. Mr. Brunton supplements here his able essay on constructive art in Japan, published in the preceding volume, by a very interesting sketch of modern Japanese architecture, sharply criticizing the want of sound judgment in the combination of sundry foreign and native styles of building and suggesting that the light and elastic style of Japanese architecture had reference to the necessities and apprehensions of earthquakes. Japanese folklore receives a valuable contribution by Mr. Goodwin's article "on some Japanese legends," exhibiting the wonderful affinity of some Japanese and European legends. This suggestion, that both were originally derived from one and the same (possibly a Turanian) source, ought to lead to further contributions on the same subject. In a paper replete with information of the highest interest for meteorologists Dr. Geert gives his observations on the climate at Nagasaki during the year 1872. Mr. Aston contributes a short account of an ancient Japanese classic (the Tosa Diary), illustrative of the manners and habits of the Japanese nearly a thousand years ago. Mr. Aston recommends this classic as a useful introduction to the study of the ancient literature of

* Copies of the works marked thus not having reached us, we quote from other reviews.

Japan. Perhaps the most interesting article in the volume before us is the one contributed by Mr. Grigsby on the Legacy of Tycyas. Whatever we may think of the authenticity of this document or of its legislative value, it certainly appears to contain the leading principles of a system which ruled Japan till quite recently, and which has given to the Japanese institutions, permeated as they are with Chinese ideas, a stamp peculiarly their own. Mr. Grigsby, being a trained Jurist, aptly illustrates this ancient document of Japanese legislature by comparisons drawn from the laws of other nations, and thus determines the place of Japan with respect to comparative Law. Mr. Dallas contributes an article on the Yonezawa dialect, valuable from a philological point of view. Interspersed with the foregoing scientific articles we find in this volume the usual number of itineraries or notes collected on excursions into the interior of Japan. Interesting as these itineraries are, especially on account of the present exclusion of foreigners from the interior, their value is considerably marred by the absence of good maps.

———

The Chinese Recorder and Missionary Journal. November-December, 1875.

Whenever we take up a number of this Journal, we find much to interest us; we read it, we study it, and profit sometimes by doing so, but we invariably put it down with a sense of disappointment. People who take up a *Missionary Journal* generally would like to know how Mission work is progressing, how the pioneers fare who are pushing their way into the interior, how many new stations and churches have been opened, how the congregations of the different Missionary Societies flourish, how Mission schools and Mission hospitals prosper, and surely in a *Missionary Journal*, if any-where, one might expect to get an answer to such questions. Missionaries always complain of the gross ignorance that prevails among Europeans in China concerning Mis-sion work, of the want of sympathy, of the signal apathy uniformly displayed by the whole foreign community up and down the China coast. But we fail to see how it possibly can be otherwise, as long as Mis-sionaries keep themselves so entirely aloof, shroud their doings in mystery, and send their reports, as it were, secretly to their respective Boards at home, whence, as we learn from Missionary evidence, these re-ports re-issue in a garbled form, cooked and touched up *couleur de rose*, to be read to and admired by people far away, when naturally distance lends enchantment to the view and the absence of local knowledge makes fair criticism an impossibility.

The foreign communities in China have far more cause to complain of the almost studied silence Missionaries generally observe with regard to their doings, and if the general verdict of public opinion that Pro-testant Missionaries on the whole are doing nothing or next to nothing is false and un-deserved, as we verily believe is the case, the blame rests on the Missionaries them-selves.

Let us take up the *Missionary Journal* before us. The present number completes the volume, and a slight improvement in the very direction we desire to indicate has been visible in the last numbers. We open this *Chinese Recorder and Missionary Journal*, and find ourselves treated to 25 pages of "Archæological and Historical Researches on Peking and its environs," a most erudite and valuable paper, like everything that

emanates from the pen of that indefatigable Sinologue, Dr. Bretschneider, who we pre-sume is not a Missionary. Next we find over 7 pages occupied with a very amusing and cleverly-written sketch of "Thieves in Mongolia" by Hoinos, who most likely is a Missionary but prefers to keep in the dark both his real name and his Missionary work. After this we alight, at last, on an article of 5 pages on "Colportage in China," giving us in homely language and artless brevity a vivid picture of four months' colportage, during which the writer travelled over more than a thousand miles and disposed of over two thousand Gospels. But leaving this pleasant oasis of Mission-ary intelligence, we have to plunge again into the desert of scientific wilderness. The Rev. J. T. Gulick contributes a short paper "on the Mandarin Mutes." This is from a philological point of view a very able essay, dealing with the usual mistake beginners make in the study of Chinese of supposing that the Chinese sounds p, t, k, or l, d, g, exactly correspond to the English mutes indicated by these letters. Mr. Gulick cor-rects Max Müller and Whitney, neither of whom, he says, notices "the difference in the method of producing the initial t and final t, for example the first t and the second t in *flat town* when pronounced together." The classification of mutes, which Mr. Gulick gives, is so convincing and so applicable to South China dialects as well as to the Man-darin dialects, that we note it here for the benefit of our readers. It is as follows:

A. Final Mutes.
1. Simple Surds—English k, t, p, as finals.
2. Close Sonants—English g, d, b, as finals.
B. Initial Mutes.
1. Explosive Surds—Mandarin k', t', p', or aspirated mutes.
2. Blown Surds—English k, t, p, as initials.
3. Open Sonants—Mandarin g' d' b' or unaspirated mutes.
4. Compound Sonants—English g, d, b, as initials.

Leaving these though dry yet passable fields of philology we are next lost in a very Sahara of trackless quicksands. The Rev.

J. L. Macilvaine, in an article on "Cushite Ethnology," volunteers to be our guide to the land of Cush. From Ethiopia, through Arabia, Babylonia and Persia, to Western India, and thence to China,—wherever on this long route he meets with a name containing the syllable "Cu," or anything like it, he will have us see in that name a trace of the wanderings of the Cushites. There is the Hindoo Koosh, designating Cush as an Indian immigrant, there is Cashmere the paradise of Cush, Calcutta the river of Cush, there were the Scythians (=Cushites) who carried a cup at their girdle, for, mark you, the Hebrew *cus*, a cup, is the basis of Cush's name! Then as to China, Mr Macilvaine produces "the most reliable form of the early Chinese tradition," his authority being the 神仙通鑑, which, as every one acquainted with Chinese literature well knows, is as reliable and trustworthy an authority as Gulliver's Travels or Herr Baron von Münchhausen. To Mr. Macilvaine however nothing comes amiss that shows a trace of the lost "Cush," and he takes for gospel-truth whatever happens to suit his theory. Well, then, the 神仙通鑑 mentioning a legendary hero, who possesses the advantage of being styled P'an-ku-shih (盤古氏), comes extremely handy. "The *ku* is a simply written character which has now and always has had the sense of 'ancient.' This sense it probably derived from its connection with this ancient man. As used in his name therefore it does not necessarily have any such meaning and may be the representation of any foreign sound, so that we do no violence in regarding it as equivalent to the *Cus* of the Hebrew. Combining it with the *shih* we have the closest approximation which the Chinese language can make to Cush. The p'an (般) is defined as a general name of all vessels for containing water, no matter of what material. The old form of the character, however, had the *metal* (金) as its radical element, instead of *vessel* (舟) as now. In this form it becomes still more significant, showing that P'an-ku

had about him some kind of a metal vessel." And among the few scores or hundreds of men then living, one Ku-shih having a metal vessel as a badge must be identified as Cush, with his golden heir-loom cup hanging at his girdle. After this our readers will not be surprised to learn that "the close study of this word *p'an* and its phonetic 般 (old form (般) creates the impression that they have to do with the ark of Noah," nor will our readers fail to be edified by "the interesting fact that in Kueicho there is a tribe called Western Miao who wear the badge of the cross and worship Thomas." But they will probably, like ourselves, fail to see anything but irreverence in Mr. Macilvaine's assertion that "the results which we have reached give us enlarged views of the Bible as the world's great *Doomsday Book*." Surely if this be "Cushite Ethnology," Ethnology itself is doomed indeed.

The remainder of the number is filled up by a short letter on "the terms for God and Spirit," a poem entitled "Thy will be done in heaven," five pages of correspondence, principally on the term Shangti for God, two pages of meagre Missionary News and six pages of "Notices of recent publications," of which but one page is devoted to the discussion of Missionary publications. Under these circumstances we cannot but call the title "Missionary Journal," which the periodical under review bears, at present a misnomer; and the Editor of that Journal, who, we have reason to know, is anxious to make his paper a thoroughly Missionary publication, may rest assured that we will give him our best assistance in the matter by keeping his contributors alive to the recognition of the duties they owe to a public so ignorant of Missionary work and its results in China.

Glimpses of Travel in the Middle Kingdom. By the Rev. Arthur Smith. Shanghai, 1875.

Under this title Mr. Smith publishes his notes of a journey from Peking to Si-ngan-foo and back. The book appears to be a reprint of articles which appeared at intervals in the *Courier*.

___

Conchyliologie Fluviatile de la Province de Nanking. * Par le R. T. Heude, de la Compagnie de Jesus, Missionaire apostolique au Kiang-Nan. Premier Fascicule. Paris, 1875.

Friends of Zoology will be interested in this first instalment of a work on the shells of Central China. The brochure is well illustrated by lithographed plates of shells of the Nayad family.

___

The Chinese Scientific Magazine, a monthly journal of popular scientific information, with which is incorporated the *Peking Magazine*. Vol. I., No. 1. Shanghai, 1876.

We are glad to see the *Peking Magazine*, which had been languishing of late, resuscitated in this form, and wish the able Editor of this new *Scientific Magazine*, Mr. J. Fryer, all success. The first number is certainly an improvement upon the old Magazine, though the letterpress leaves much yet to be desired.

___

The Eastern Seas: * being a Narrative of the Voyage of H.M. Ship *Dwarf* in China, Japan and Formosa. By Captain B. W. Bax, R.N. London, John Murray, 1875.

This is a collection of desultory notes compiled in the course of many desultory cruises of the well-known gunboat *Dwarf*. It is however well worth the attention of those who are interested in the progress which the Chinese and Japanese have lately been making in the art of war. Captain Bax visited the Foochow Arsenal, examined many of the Chinese gunboats and watched Chinese marines at their gun-drill; he had also opportunities to observe the Japanese navy and the foreign-drilled portion of their army which put down the revolt at Saga, and he states the result of his observations

in pleasant and forcible language. He has formed a high opinion of the capabilities of both the Chinese and Japanese navy, and thinks that the Chinese especially require but an efficient system for training cadets and commanders in whom their crews can have confidence to make their gunboats really formidable. The book throws also new light on the progress the Russians are making with their system of strategical colonization of the territories situated at the mouth of the Amur and in Eastern Siberia with a view of establishing themselves in a commanding position in the event of their being involved in troubles with China or Japan.

___

A meeting of the Asiatic Society of Japan was held on January 5th, at which a paper on the *Winds and Currents of Japan*, by Captain David Scott, was read, and this was supplemented by some tabular statements on the temperature of the water at the different ports of Japan and at Vladivostok by Mr. J. W. Dupen of H. M. S. *Ringdove*. The whole paper consisted of useful notes on the subjects of the Winds and Currents. On the latter topic Mr. Dupen's paper generally agreed with the notes of Captain Scott.

At a meeting of the same Society held on 19th January, Mr. H. Brunton read a series of notes taken during a visit to Okinawa-Shima, one of the Loochow islands.

___

We learn with regret that the well-known Botanist, Dr. Savatier, the accomplished author of the "Enumeratio plantarum in Japonia sponte crescentium," had to return to France, leaving the great work he had set himself, and which he has thus far so admirably executed, but half accomplished. It is highly desirable that the French Government should assist so eminent a Botanist in reaping for himself and his country the full honour of his patient and long-continued researches.

___

We have seen some extremely well executed maps of Eastern Asia, including the whole of China Proper, Manchuria, Corea and Japan. These maps appear to have been executed by the Topographical Bureau of the Japanese War Office. All the letterpress is done in the Chinese character with admirable neatness and precision. These maps are really a marvel of workmanship. The only fault we have to find with them is that the size is too large for a map of reference, and the letterpress too fine for a wall map.

———

A meeting of the North China Branch of the R. A. S. took place in Shanghai on 1st February, when Mr. Kingsmill, after referring to a former paper of his on the Chow dynasty which he correctly designated as "a crude attempt to fathom the mythical origin of Chinese history" and to his notes on the legend of Yaou published a few months ago in the *Celestial Empire*, read a paper on "the Story of the Emperor Shun." We have no more faith than Mr. Kingsmill himself has in the credibility of the records of early Chinese history, and we are so far delighted to see Mr. Kingsmill persevere in his endeavours to prove the mythical character of all the ancient Chinese heroes. But we have grave doubts as to the soundness of his view that Chinese mythology is altogether derived from Indian sources. We were often surprised to find the members of the Shanghai Asiatic Society acquiesce in Mr. Kingsmill's crude speculations, and it is therefore a matter of gratification to us to learn that Mr. Wylie, than whom none of the resident members was more fit to pronounce a judgment, at last overcame at this meeting his characteristic modesty and ventured to enter a feeble protest. He himself, Mr Wylie said, could not form an opinion on the subject, not being well acquainted with the mythology of the period or of that with which it is compared. He thought philology was an unsafe guide, as so much

depended upon sounds, and he had noticed that in many of the myths which were compared in different countries even the words bore no resemblance. He asked, did the Chinese work the myths into history? If the whole history of the Shoo-king be a myth, where are we to look for its origin, in India or in China? Might it not have passed as history from China into India, and there have assumed its mythical shape?

———

We learn from the *China Express* that Mr. F. B. Forbes, of Shanghai, now in Europe, is preparing an enumeration of all the *Phænerogamia* and *Filices* hitherto discovered in China Proper. It is to be hoped that he will publish it, for, with the exception of Bentham's *Flora Hongkongensis*, the literature of Chinese botany is very widely scattered, and many species still remain undescribed. We understand that the *Phanerogamia* represented in the Herbarium at Kew number about 3,000 species, including those from the Korea and Formosa, and the *Filices* a little more than 200 species. These figures are, perhaps, scarcely so high as might have been anticipated, but it should be remembered that successive collectors have trodden nearly the same ground, and the botany of many of the interior provinces is still practically unknown. The recent collections of the Abbé Armand David and Dr. Bushell in North China, or of Dr. Shearer, Kiukiang, and those of the Yunnan expedition made by Dr. Anderson, though small, go to prove that China still offers a rich booty to the botanical traveller.

———

The Rev. J. Edkins, D.D., the well-known author of "China's Place in Philology," has just returned to China. His new works, "An Introduction to the study of the Chinese character," will be published within a few weeks from this by Messrs Trübner & Co.

NOTES AND QUERIES.

NOTES.

CHINESE ANTI-OPIUM ASSOCIATIONS.— Both in Hongkong and Canton local associations have lately been formed by natives for the purpose of composing and publishing tracts and placards with a view to warn the people against the evils of opium smoking. We have seen several such placards issued by the Canton Association. The Hongkong Anti-Opium Society has not yet, as far as we are aware, published anything, and we are curious to see what this Society has to say on the subject, as we understand the local Opium Farmer is himself a member of the local Anti-Opium Society's Committee.

PUBLICATIONS OF THE HONGKONG CORRESPONDING COMMITTEE OF THE RELIGIOUS TRACT SOCIETY.—We are informed that during the past year a considerable number of new books have been issued by this Committee in the Chinese language. We especially note that the Rev. E. Faber's "Sermons on Mark" are now completed in four good-sized volumes. A new tract in one volume on the subject of Geomancy, from the pen of the Rev. Wan-wai-ts'ing, has been issued, and a reprint of Mr. Chalmers' well-known pamphlet "on the name of God" (正名要論) is in the press.

HONGKONG SCHOOL-BOOK COMMITTEE.— We are glad to learn that this Committee, appointed some years ago by the Hongkong Government for the purpose of preparing a series of Chinese School-books, to be used in the local schools with a view to supplement the study of the Chinese classics by books supplying materials for secular instruction, have just completed their Third Reading Book, which will shortly be issued.

An Oriental series entitled "Bibliothèque de l'Ecole des Langues Orientales," has just been commenced under the auspices of the French Ministry of Public Instruction, which contributes a very liberal subsidy to the undertaking. The first work of the series is an edition of Mir Abd-ul-Kerim's "Description of Afghanistan, Bokhara, and Khiva," by M. Charles Schefer, official interpreter to the French Government. The Persian text, which for typographical reasons has been printed at Bulak, in Egypt, is ready for distribution. The French translation has just gone to press, and will fill about three hundred large octavo pages; it will be accompanied by a handsome map of Central Asia. The publisher of the series is M. Ernest Leroux.

M. de Mohl, an Orientalist scholar, died recently in Paris. He began the study of theology at Tubingen, but, feeling a decided vocation for the study of languages, he came to England, where he made the acquaintance of several distinguished Orientalists, and thence to Paris, where he became the pupil and friend of Abel de Rémusat. He published a Latin translation of the "Y-king," and from 1833 to 1855 he gave the celebrated Persian poem of "Chah-Namch."

In 1847 he succeeded M. Jaubert as professor of Persian at the College de France, and his writings have done much to popularise the study of Oriental languages in Paris.

It is stated that Mr. Clements Markham, in the course of his researches in connection with the forthcoming work on Tibet, which he is engaged in editing under the orders of the Secretary of State for India, has succeeded in unearthing, at Middelburg, in Holland, particulars respecting a great Dutch traveller named Samuel Van Del Putte, the only European who has ever made his way from India by way of Tibet to China.

The University of Oxford is about to sustain a loss in its professorial staff, which it cannot but find well-nigh impossible to repair. Mr. Max Müller has announced that after twenty-six years of indefatigable, and it must be added successful, academical labours he is about to retire from active working and teaching, and intends to devote the residue of his days to the completion of his *magnum opus*, "the text, commentary, and translation of the oldest of the sacred books of the Brahmans, the oldest book of the Aryan world, the most ancient and most important monument of Sanskrit literature." The greater portion of this task he has already finished. In addition to his professorial duties he has printed at the University Press what would amount to a volume of about six hundred pages octavo of pure Sanskrit in every one of the last twenty-five years. Even now there are seven more volumes of Brahman hymns to be edited and published, in addition to sundry minor agenda which Professor Max Müller does not particularise.

We hear that Dr. Legge has been engaged for some months on the revision of the *Shêking*, which he will shortly issue in English verse. It will be interesting to note the work in this form, conforming it to the style in the original, in which it may

have a more engaging appearance than in its present prosaic dress.

Mr. Groeneveldt is engaged in the compilation of a History of Trans-Gangetic India (Annam, Cambodgia, Siam and Burmah) from Chinese sources. The work is to be published in French.

Baron von Richthofen, lately appointed Professor of Geography at the University of Bonn, is still busy preparing for the press a resume of his researches into Chinese topography.

QUERIES.

CHINESE WILLS.—On a recent occasion Sir John Smale, Chief Justice of Hongkong, seemed to be puzzled by the difficulties he experienced in extracting from the native interpreters and other officers of the Court a decided opinion as to Chinese practice in the matter of wills. In the case before Sir John Smale the question arose whether, according to Chinese custom, a will having but one subscribing witness is valid. Can any of the readers of the *China Review* refer me to some Chinese work dealing with the subject of wills, or to some authority showing how wills should be executed and attested; or can any one at least tell me what is the custom on the subject in the Canton Province?
E. J. E.

CHINESE BREECH-LOADING GUNS.—I have occasionally seen breech-loading guns at Mandarin Yaméns and on board of Junks. It appears that with each gun there are four or five breech pieces (or blocks) into which the charge of powder and the bullet is inserted by an assistant; it is then put into its place in the breech of the gun and then retained by an iron wedge driven in by a heavy mallet or hammer; the charge is ignited by means of a slow match or joss stick. Can any of your readers tell at about what period this gun was first used by the Chinese?
J. C.

HISTORY OF THE MARITIME PROVINCES.— What has become of the History of the Maritime Provinces of China which, contributed by the joint industry of the various Commissioners of Customs, was to have appeared from the Customs press long since ? Crumbs from the promised loaf have occasionally appeared in our pages, and several interesting episodes of the histories of both Amoy and Canton have been set before our readers. But these, interesting and pleasing as we trust they have been found, have merely served to whet curiosity in scholarly circles and to raise expectations which are not yet fulfilled. If the work be at all similar in its general character to what has already appeared, it ought not, even though it be incomplete, to be withheld from the literary public. And if it be throughout as painstaking and carefully compiled as those contributions which we have been allowed to see, we venture to predict that it will be a book of no ordinary interest.

N. N.

BOOKS WANTED, EXCHANGES, &c.

(All addresses to care of Editor, *China Review.*)

BOOKS WANTED.

The undersigned wants a printed or manuscript copy of the following books, 島夷志畧, 安南志畧, 越史畧 and 変州記, the three first of which are mentioned in Wylie's Bibliography respectively on p. 47 and 33. He would feel greatly obliged if any readers of the *China Review* would assist him in procuring these works.

W. P. G.

Li-ki on Mémorial des Rites, traduit pour la première fois du Chinois et accompagné de notes, de commentaires et du texte original, par J. M. Callery. Turin, 1853.

Address, H. K.

FOR SALE.

Morrison's Dictionary, 6 vols. complete (large edition), price $20.

Address, X.

TO PURCHASE OR EXCHANGE.

Endliches Verzeichniss der Chinesischen und Japanischen Münzen des K. K. Münz, and Antiken-Cabinetes in Wien 1837, 8vo.

Native Treatises on Numismatics.

A Collection of Bank Notes issued by the Daimios of Japan.

Rare Chinese and Japanese Coins.

Address, A.
(Hongkong.)

www.ingramcontent.com/pod-product-compliance
Lightning Source LLC
Chambersburg PA
CBHW022024080426
42733CB00007B/721